HIRED FOR LIFE

HIRED FOR LIFE

CHRISTOPHER WEBER

NEW DEGREE PRESS

HIRED FOR LIFE

ISBN 978-1-64137-258-9 *Paperback*

978-1-64137-259-6 *Ebook*

CONTENTS

	ACKNOWLEDGEMENTS	7
	INTRODUCTION	11
PART 1.	**THE LANDSCAPE**	**25**
CHAPTER 1.	THE NEW LANDSCAPE	27
CHAPTER 2.	TODAY'S EMPLOYEES	49
PART 2.	**THE H4L FOUNDATION**	**63**
CHAPTER 3.	HONESTY	65
CHAPTER 4.	INNER AWARENESS	87
CHAPTER 5.	REMOVING ANXIETY	101
CHAPTER 6.	ENGAGING ALUMNI	119
CHAPTER 7.	DEMONSTRATION	131
PART 3.	**THE ROADMAP**	**149**
CHAPTER 8.	THE H4L ORGANIZATION	151
CHAPTER 9.	H4L IN ACTION	169

PART 4.	**THE H4L EXECUTION**	**191**
CHAPTER 10.	CAREER CONVERSATIONS	193
CHAPTER 11.	PERFORMANCE CONVERSATIONS	209
CHAPTER 12.	THE PLAYBOOK	229
CHAPTER 13.	JOB CRAFTING	241
CHAPTER 14.	THE LONG GAME	257
	BIBLIOGRAPHY	271

ACKNOWLEDGEMENTS

First and foremost I would like to thank my wife, Kristin. You have always trusted me, and it has made all the difference. I love you. Adeline, Emily, Mom, Dad, and Bob, thank you for always supporting me, and for making me a better person. I love you all.

Thank you to everyone I interviewed for this book. The insights drawn from your words will certainly help the next generation of great professionals. And thank you to everyone who reviewed these pages to make it better.

Thank you to everyone at New Degree Press, including Brian, Leila, Hazel, Gjorgji, and the rest for keeping me on track through this crazy journey.

Finally, this wouldn't have happened with Eric Koester. Thanks for always making me feel like I was the only author you were working with. I don't know how you do it.

This book is a work of nonfiction. It reflects the author's present recollections of experiences over time. Some names and characteristics have been changed, some events have been compressed, and some dialogue has been recreated.

INTRODUCTION

While attending evening law school, I started my legal career as a Student Associate at an internationally renowned intellectual property firm. There, I worked with countless partners and associates, some of whom remain in my life today. Four months after my first daughter was born, and eight months before law school graduation, however, like so many others during the great recession, I found out that I was losing my job.

Years later, I welcomed the opportunity to work with partners from that firm again. You see, whether they knew it or not, those partners hired me for life.

**

The U.S. is known for many things, but one of the things we are the envy of the world is our robust and vibrant professional services economy.

In a clearly advertorial message, the U.S. Department of Commerce shares, "The United States is the world's most desired location for professional services firms. In today's integrated global environment, businesses find it critical to access the talent, institutions, business processes, and client base offered in the United States. Additionally, the educational and research infrastructure present in the United States is an important asset for domestic and international professional services firms."[1]

They aren't wrong. The U.S. is certainly good at professional services and I should know, I've spent nearly a decade deep in this sector.

Let's first start by defining what exactly is the professional services industry:

Professional Services can generally be defined as occupations requiring special training in the arts or sciences and include

1 "Professional Services Industry Spotlight | Selectusa.Gov". 2019. *Selectusa.Gov*. Accessed June 25 2019. https://www.selectusa.gov/professional-services-industry-united-states.

the services of lawyers, accountants, architects, engineers, doctors and dentists.[2]

For the purpose of this book, we'll eliminate doctors and dentists that rightfully are better described as medical professionals. We'll be focusing on the other categories of professionals including the lawyers, accountants, management consultants, and engineering firms. It's actually a huge part of our economy, generating annual revenue of $1.76 trillion in 2017, a 2.1 percent increase from 2016, and employing 9 million people across nearly 1.2 million firms.[3]

Some of the most storied and prestigious organizations in the world are a part of this booming sector of the economy, such as Goldman Sachs, McKinsey & Co., Bain, IBM, DLA Piper, Jones Day, KMPG, PriceWaterhouseCoopers, and Davis Polk, among others.

These organizations are often the first career stop for the best and the brightest college graduates — and rightfully so — most college students have long been told that the long hours and hard work is worth it to become a partner some day. But even if you don't, the saying goes, you're likely setup for a successful career because you got your start at one of

2 Ibid.

3 Ibid.

these firms. Today, however, there's a more common refrain you'll hear if you are out for drinks with these young, ambitious new professional firm employees:

"It's good experience and good money. But no, I'm not interested in going for partner."

Times they are a changin'.

**

Historically, professional services firms have leveraged the partnership business model. This is a model built around the principle of promoting people from within the company to a "partner" level. It's usually a fairly arduous journey, often averaging around a decade with various steps and stages. But it's the carrot for the challenging early parts of the job: big salary, sharing of profits and the power of leverage from junior staff. This is the brass ring.

Once the individual is promoted to partner level they are expected to tackle key leadership roles, manage others, take on more responsibility for developing the business, and play a key role in the firm's growth.

And what about those that don't make it to, or choose to reach for the, partner title?

"Up or out," is typically the message.

What does that mean? Well, it means that professional services firms organizationally are built like a pyramid. Essentially, there are fewer partners than associates, staff accountants, and analysts. The model works around a concept known as "leverage" — how many non-partners partners 'leverage' for their top-level work. There is an entire strategic world that analyzes and optimizes how the right mixture of partner-level, senior-level, middle-level, and junior-level resources affects the firm's profitability and growth.

But perhaps more crassly put—leverage is all about 'up or out' meaning you either get promoted 'up' to partner or you find the door.

For me, like most every junior employee at a professional services firm, I found the door—Twice.

**

"Congrats on your offer!" I said to just about every one of my fellow students associates (a position unique to patent law firms, essentially full time summer associates who work during the day and go to school at night).

"Thanks!" they all replied, followed by, a slightly gloomier, "Have you heard anything yet?"

I had not heard anything yet. Not the Monday after they got their offers on Friday, nor the rest of the week. Not the next week. And not the week after.

"No sense in asking. No sense is speeding up my exit."

"No, you'll still hear something. You were the only one in your technology for our class. So that group must just be delayed."

It was nice for them to say. But they knew. I knew. Everyone gets offers on the same day so no one worries about their future.

In fact, when a friend of mine's class got their offers, his cohorts got theirs on a Thursday, and he didn't get his until Friday morning. When the hiring partner called him into his office on Friday, he spent the first 10 minutes apologizing for not talking to him Thursday. The day had gotten away from him and some variety of work/family emergency came up at the end of the day.

"I can't imagine how bad it must have been for you last night. I'm sure you knew the others got their offers yesterday. I'm so sorry."

12 hours? I waited three weeks.

Here's the thing. I understood! The economy was in the dumps. And many firms were in trouble. It wasn't just firms reporting lower profits. There was a news story about a firm closing weekly. Industry-wide there were salary freezes, bonus reductions, summer associates not getting offers (something that is historically unheard of), and of course layoffs.

I'd be lying if I said I didn't want, or wasn't expecting, an offer. It hurt not to get one and had an obvious impact on my life. But like I said, I understood. I just wished that the message was delivered better. The delivery is sometimes as important as the message itself.

**

This book is not a jaded missive from a bitter employee who lost out on the partnership track or who felt under appreciated for his time at any of the professional services firms that employed me. Elite firms are stacked with talent, top to bottom, and many do a fantastic job preparing associates for future jobs throughout the industry. Every firm I worked at taught me the skills I needed to progress in my legal career, even if it wasn't at the firm where I learned it.

I also both appreciate the partnership organizational model and pathway to partner. In fact, I've not found anything that tells me there's a better alternative. I think it's likely the best and most efficient business model for professional services firms.

I'll argue that 'If it ain't broke, don't try to fix it.'

But I think professional services firms — and their associates — are missing a huge opportunity:

Hiring for Life.

Over the past several years, I've studied, researched and interviewed hundreds of former employees of professional services firms — accountants, lawyers, engineers, architects, and consultants.For the most part, they all appreciate the partnership model. Some are bitterer about their outcomes from the race than others. But very few felt as if they got something different than they bargained for.

We all "appreciate" the limits of the model of professional services firms.

But something else struck me about these conversations: certain individuals were downright effusive of praise of their prior employers. It was the kind of praise that felt almost fake at first blush — like something that makes you feel like you're hearing someone talk about a cult or Amway (which might say something about Amway).

Certain professional services alums had a unique and different relationship with their employers.

They were hired for life — I just didn't know that's what it was at the time.

This book offers a unique framework that the best professional services firms and managers have created to hire employees for life. The Hired for Life principles manifest themselves in this unique connection to a firm that fired you, politely showed you the door, or that you choose to leave. Think of it like being best friends with your former spouse after a divorce.

It just seems weird, right?

But it's not. In fact, it's the single greatest advantage a professional services firm can have in today's world.

It's literally a multi-billion dollar secret right in front of our eyes...and 99.9% of us have missed it.

Hired for Life = H4L

**

This book will feature stories and insights including:

- How a common characteristic between an NBA player and local lawyer resulted in both becoming irreplaceable rockstars, despite not being traditional superstars;
- How a startup uses meaningful games and activities beyond the clichéd trust fall to demonstrate H4L culture and build relationships among employees;
- How a mid-size firm uses career conversations to ensure associates know early and often that opportunities are available to anyone who is interested in operating as a partner, what those opportunities are, and what the expectations are for succeeding at those opportunities;
- How an advice letter system from a big law firm, combined with a manager overview system from a big consulting firm can combine to build a powerful playbook for associates to quickly integrate to a firm by knowing on day one the in and outs of the firm and its partners; and
- How every single associate that walks through the firms front door, is either a potential future partner, future collaborator, or, most importantly, future client.

I will detail a unique framework that these organizations and managers have implemented to create the relationships that ultimately lead to this unfair advantage.

Hired for Life is laid out as follows:

Part I – The Landscape – Discussion of the new workplace landscape and the new considerations for today's employees.

Part II – The Foundation – Detailing the H4L principles that conveniently spell out H-I-R-E-D:

H onesty
I nner Awareness
R emoving of Anxiety
E ngaging Alumni
D emonstration

Part III – The Roadmap – Exemplary stories highlighting the foundational principles from Part II and the tactical principles from Part IV.

Part IV – The Execution – Detailing the tactical principles of H4L.

**

Whom is Hired for Life for?

As I'll discuss, H4L works best when all three elements in the organization buy in: Culture – Management – Employees.

Therefore, all three would benefit from understanding the principles.

Fundamentally, because an organization must choose to implement H4L, Hired for Life generally is directed towards those who direct the organization's Culture (Talent Acquisition and Retention; Management Committee, Practice Group Leaders) and Management (Any partners, of counsel, and senior associates who manage professionals).

Let's start there.

Why should you even care whether your firm is an H4L organization or not? Can't you just do good work and count on the referral of the clients with whom you work?

In fact, 82% of referrals come from people who have never worked with you as a client.[4] That's right, referrals are driven by non-client advocates. The biggest insight and take away from H4L employees is that nearly every one of them has themselves hired their former employer — even if they were fired by the firm — or they've strongly recommended the firm that previously employed them.

"Oh, you used to work there... what are your thoughts?"

---

4 Ibid.

How your former employees answer that question, who most likely are active in your industry or profession now, albeit in a different capacity, is the difference between rapid growth and stagnation. In the world of professional services firms, you'll often see your former employees going on to become the head of strategy or general counsel or chief financial officer at a Fortune 50 company who just happens to need to hire a management consulting firm, a law firm to handle some litigation, or a new accounting firm, respectively.

H4L is critical in a world where your employees are your clients and friends of your clients. Just sometimes, that road takes a decade or more to pay off for the H4L employer.

And lest you think this book is just for partners and managers at firms, H4L is a principle every professional should deeply understand and leverage. Can't you just do good work and count on making partner? Statistically, no. Odds are you won't become partner and maybe there are unique roles (non-equity partner or some derivation), but don't count on that.

But as an associate, you have a potentially much bigger role to play: Future Client.

You should plan to be more "out" than "up," so finding a firm that'll create an 'out' path that leads you on a new and different path to success is critical. This book is designed to assist employees without partnership ambitions — the best candidates for H4L firms — to identify and navigate their pathway to and through H4L organizations and managers.

**

Everyday throughout the professional services industry, a former firm approaches a former associate to bid on work. That work could represent hundreds of thousands of dollars, to millions of dollars, directly to those firms. Moreover, former associates like me recommend former firms, often-specific partners, and associates, dozens of times in serious buying conversations. Thus, it is my hope that every professional, regardless of position or status, understands and commits to the principles of H4L, even if your organization does not.

PART I

THE LANDSCAPE

CHAPTER 1

THE NEW LANDSCAPE

"[Managers] worried that the tour of duty framework might give employees "permission" to leave. But permission is not yours to give or to withhold, and believing you have that power is simply a self-deception that leads to a dishonest relationship with your employees. Employees don't need your permission to switch companies, and if you try to assert that right, they'll simply make their move behind your back."[5]

Let that sink in.

That's from *The Alliance*, by Reid Hoffman, Ben Casnocha, and Chris Yeh.

---

5 Hoffman, Reid, Chris Yeh, and Ben Casnocha. 2013. *The Alliance*. London: HarperCollins.

This quote brings to mind a story a mid-level associate, Sam, told me about a conversation she had with a partner when a junior professional told the firm he wanted to leave to go to a different firm.

"It's so annoying when someone tells us they want to leave AFTER they accept an offer. It makes it so much harder for us to convince them to stay because they feel obligated to the new firm."

The partner was obviously annoyed, so Sam probed a little.

"Well, he probably assumes that as soon as he tells you he's interested in leaving that you'll assume he's damaged goods or something. So might as well just commit to leaving, get the offer, then tell you."

"Nope. We try to help. If someone wants to go in-house, maybe we'll have a connection for them. Or if they think they need to go to another firm, we would try to get them to stay."

Intriguing.

"Why is that?" Sam asked.

"It pisses me off when someone leaves to go to another firm."

"Because you're sorry to see them go?"

"No! How crappy is it that we spend all this time, effort, and money to train someone to have them go compete with us?!"

On one hand, this is completely understandable. Finding and training any new employee is expensive. And associates can be more expensive than others based on lost billable hours during ramp up periods and low early billing rates relative to salaries.

But on the other hand, and this is a drum I'm going to beat throughout Hired for Life, they are going to leave anyway. H4L is about making that exit event worthwhile.

**

Times, they are a changin'.

When I look at the trajectory of the American corporation from the industrial revolution, I see two big themes with associates' changes.

First, the shift from the model of "business is a family" to "employees are 'free agents'." This shift is covered extensively in *The Alliance*:

"The traditional model of lifetime employment, so well-suited to periods of relative stability, is too rigid for today's networked age. Few American companies can provide the traditional career ladder for their employees anymore; the model is in varying degrees of disarray globally."[6]

Second, and what I see as at least part of the reason for the first big shift, the increased importance of information relative to personnel.

Compare the following quotes:

"The seminal difference between successful companies and mediocre or unsuccessful ones has little, if anything, to do with what they know or how smart they are; it has everything to do with how healthy they are."[7]

"During the Industrial Revolution, companies achieved competitive advantage by substituting machines for human labor. Information processing at that time was mostly the result of human effort. Now the pace of technological change is reversed. This technological transformation is expanding the limits of what companies can do faster than managers can

---

6 Ibid.

7 Lencioni, Patrick. 2012. *The Advantage*. San Francisco: Jossey-Bass.

explore the opportunities. This new technology substitutes machines for human effort in information processing."[8]

The first feels to me like something Henry Ford would have said. The second, the kind of soulless thing you would expect to hear in our modern era of replacing even more humans with machines.

In fact, the second quote is from a 1985 article in the *Harvard Business Review* by Michael Porter and Victor Millar titled "How Information Gives You Competitive Advantage." And the first quote is from *The Advantage*. Written in 2012 by Patrick Lencioni during the thick of another high tech boom, a time tech startups who are allegedly trying to destroy everything that was good about things "back in the day."

So what happened? Have we come full circle?

No, not quite, we still aren't back to "family." I agree with *The Alliance* that it's not where things are or should be headed. At least not with how we define "family," but maybe we should shift back to an employee focus.

**

8 Porter, Michael, and Victor Millar. 1985. "How Information Gives You Competitive Advantage". *Harvard Business Review*. https://hbr.org/1985/07/how-information-gives-you-competitive-advantage.

Captain Obvious' statement of the book: H4L works best with buy-in from all three core elements of the organization:

Culture – Manager – Employee

While three is ideal, in some cases, two out of three will work, but there will be consequences and quirks.

For example:

Culture + Manager – Organization may lose short-term benefits due to lack of employee buy-in during the employee's tenure. However, long-term benefits to the organization are still possible if and when the employee/ex-employee realizes the benefits later.

Manager + Employee – Organization will gain short-term benefits due to employee buy-in during the employee's tenure. Yet, it may lose long-term benefits because the employee's loyalty and good will is directed to the manager, not the organization.

Culture + Employee – This is the most challenging and underscores the importance of manager buy-in. Organization may lose short-term benefits because the employee is not growing sufficiently under poor management. Nevertheless, there is still potential for long-term benefits from the employee, if that employee makes a positive impression to other managers. A common situation here would be an associate who works with multiple partners.

In each case, there is a reason for the employee not to recommend the firm, either short or long-term. When all three are present, however, those reasons go away.

Culture + Manager + Employee – Organization will gain short-term benefits from happy skillful employees. Moreover, the organization will gain long-term benefits from the former employees who credit, not only their manager, but also the organization with their success.

**

The professional services industry is set up so perfectly for H4L; it is really quite surprising it hasn't naturally just happened.

Think about it.

- There are an incredibly large amount of firms to choose from, each at different price points and specialties.
- The firms at the higher end rely on natural attrition to keep the business model working.

- With ever escalating billing rates, there are certain clients that bigger firms will simply never be able to (or want to) take on.
- There are clients that smaller firms simply do not have the capacity to service.
- And all firms rely heavily on referrals to build business.

So why aren't the concepts of H4L formally present throughout the professional services industry?

I think it has a lot to do with the fact that subject matter experts are not necessarily trained to be managers or leaders. Or that they even want to be managers or leaders!

**

If you're a partner reading this, you've probably laughed over a bourbon thinking about this next quote (or maybe even said it yourself back in the day!), and if you're an associate, you've probably said it, or heard it. I'll note that the veracity of this quote isn't relevant, the perception is there.

"Why don't the partners treat associates better?"

If a more junior associate is saying this to a more senior associate, the response might be"

"Don't forget, we're a fungible resource."

Let's do a quick refresher on the definition of fungible:

"Fungible – being something (such as money or a commodity) of such a nature that one part or quantity may be replaced by another equal part or quantity in paying a debt or settling an account."[9]

The conversation might continue with, "Ok, fine. But is that really good business to treat us that way?"

"They didn't go to law school because they wanted to be business people."

Ding. Ding. Ding.

**

"I've never understood the model where client-facing managing partners have to give up elements of their portfolio and get loaded with more management."[10]

---

9 "Definition Of FUNGIBLE". 2019. *Merriam-Webster.Com*. https://www.merriam-webster.com/dictionary/fungible.

10 Martindale, Nick. 2014. "Partnership Management Model Outdated?". *Economia.Icaew.Com*. https://economia.icaew.com/features/march-2014/shift-away-from-partnership-model.

That's Jonathan Fox, managing partner at SafferyChampness, from Nick Martindale's 2014 *Economia* article,"Partnership management model outdated?" SafferyChampness is a top accountancy firm in the UK.

Fox is *not* an accountant.

"I wasn't recruited to be a managing partner; I was recruited to be an executive partner to support a client-facing managing partner," Fox continues.[11]

Translation: Let me handle some of the management, so that you can keep billing.

Martindale also found that it's just not bigger firms that are experimenting with these types of arrangements.

Martindale interviewed Simon Brownbill, who "is a partner and director of practice development at Manchester firm HURST – with 70 people including 13 partners, and three offices." Brownbill "originally joined as marketing director."[12]

As Brownbill tells it: "I quickly took on a range of other responsibilities that included business development, HR,

---

11 Ibid.
12 Ibid.

customer services, our international business plan, and other income lines. I also look after strategic projects such as new office set-ups."[13]

At HURST, "Fee-earning partners remain involved on the commercial side, but Brownbill sees his role as helping to co-ordinate that and ensure it doesn't adversely impact on the day job. 'Before I was here, they all realised they needed to do business development; some were good at it and some were bad at it,' he says. 'Consequently, some of the clients we brought in were good and some were bad, and we'd end up under-servicing some and over-servicing others. It was a mess.'"[14]

It's interesting to compare how most professional service firms operate relative to a traditional product-based company works: specifically smaller and/or startup firms.

At a traditional startup, it's incredibly common for a founder to hire a CEO/President to actually run their company. Hire salespeople to go out and sell their product or service. Have a group that is in charge of real estate that builds out locations. And so on.

---

13 Ibid.
14 Ibid.

But at firms, even as they get larger, partners are regularly involved in how the firm runs, selling the firm's services, and doing things such as choosing what kind of furniture to use in the new office.

Do you know what else partners are doing? Building culture. Setting up performance metrics. Figuring out retention strategies. In other words, trying to do things that might be outside of their expertise. In fact, the list could include quite a lot of things that require a different skill set than arguing in front of court, designing a skyscraper, or inventing a new overseas tax strategy.

Not everyone agrees of course. Martindale certainly ran into skeptics. Who said things like:

"As accountants, we like to think we know how to run a business."[15]

This skeptic, Stephen Corner from Barnes Roffe does have a point with respect to client relationships.

---

15 Ibid.

"We can't get away from the fact that our clients are not numbers and that our business at the level we are is based on personal relationships."[16]

I actually agree with this.

But...

As Ray Dalio says:

"Get to know your blind spots."

I think that at many firms the mismanagement of associates is a *massive* blind spot.

**

A component of this mismanagement is thinking of associates as a fungible resource—a collection of billable hours.

A critical element of being fungible is that any particular unit of the resource is nameless, faceless. A barrel of oil is like any other barrel of oil. A 4th year billable hour is the same as any other 4th year billable hour.

---

16 Ibid.

The difference is that when you sell the barrel of oil, you get your $50 wholesale price and then you never see it again.

But when an associate leaves, that associate's potential impact is far from over. You don't *just* get the hours the associate billed while they were there, you get the hours they refer. You also lose the hours they don't refer, or worse, deter.

Back to nameless and faceless for a second. When you reduce an associate to a collection of billable hours, it's easy to see how that starts to look a lot like the associates are nothing more than a collection of knowledge . . . data . . . information.

Revisiting the quote from the *Harvard Business Review*: "During the Industrial Revolution, companies achieved competitive advantage by substituting machines for human labor."[17]

The problem with associate labor is that you can't really replace it with a machine. Well, at least not with a literal machine. But you can sure try to turn that human associate into a figurative machine.

"So and so is a machine."

---

17 Porter, Michael, and Victor Millar. 1985. "How Information Gives You Competitive Advantage". *Harvard Business Review*. https://hbr.org/1985/07/how-information-gives-you-competitive-advantage.

"That associate can just crank away for hours."

The Advantage proposes that organizational health trumps information, and I would add "automation with human."

Does the current professional services firm model seem very healthy?

**

The principles of H4L – Honesty, Inner Awareness, Removing Anxiety, Engaging Alumni, and Demonstration – require humans to interact with humans.

So maybe we should start by getting to know each other better?

**

Lencioni tells a story in *The Advantage* about just this topic:

"During an off-site session, we take teams through a quick exercise where we ask them to tell everyone, briefly, a few things about their lives. . . . . [W]e're not interested in their inner childhoods, just what was uniquely challenging for them growing up.

"This inevitably leads to a newly found sense of respect because of the admiration that comes when someone realizes that one of their peers endured and overcame a hardship or accomplished something remarkable."[18]

I know it's silly, but I think about what goes through my head when someone cuts me off in traffic. The easy explanation is that person is a jerk. And I'll concede that is likely the case. But do you really know? How can you know what motivates a person? Whether or not it's excusable, maybe they are rushing to the hospital to get to a loved one. Maybe they just had a bad day at work. You can't know unless you ask.

The notion of vulnerability will be discussed throughout this book as well, and it comes up in Lencioni's story.

"In addition to making people feel more comfortable being vulnerable, this discussion serves to level the playing field on the team. I always find it amazing to witness how quickly the dynamic of a team can change after a simple twenty-minute exercise as people who thought they knew one another develop a whole new level of respect, admiration, and understanding, regardless of their job title, age, or experience."[19]

---

18 Lencioni, Patrick. 2012. *The Advantage*. San Francisco: Jossey-Bass.
19 Ibid.

During one of these exercises, the CFO described his upbringing.

"He had no indoor plumbing during part of his childhood, and the electrical service in his home was inconsistent at best. You'd have thought the guy grew up during the 1850s."[20]

And that CFO's quote at the end of his personal story is the kicker.

"So that's probably why I'm so tight with the money."[21]

How would we treat people if we knew a little more about them?

**

"So, just so that I fully understand, are you going to be able to work on the motion for summary judgement tonight or not?"

That line was delivered, by a partner, to Connor while he was laying in a hospital bed after being admitted to the hospital for an indefinite amount of time, but at least a week.

---

20 Ibid.

21 Ibid.

As Connor told me, "It had been a pretty intense couple of days. We were all working long and hard to get the motion ready. I'm fine with the roller coaster schedule that litigation can be. I knew what I was getting into.

"I certainly didn't plan on having an appendicitis [attack] the night before the motion was due. I managed to send an email to the team letting them know that I was being admitted and would be in the hospital for a couple days.

"I mostly got back well wishes. I didn't realize that I had to be more specific about whether I would be able to work while in the E.R."

Maybe that's what this partner would have said to their best friend. But I don't think so. And I don't even think this partner was being particularly cold hearted. Maybe he or she was just reading the email too fast. But more likely the partner was just thinking about the motion first and the associate second.

It would be like if your car broke down "can we get it fixed in time for us to make it to the concert?" That is the danger of thinking of associates as resources.

And I have been in these situations before, and it's terrible. But again, maybe it's about the delivery of the message.

Everyone knows the work has to get done. Maybe the email instead reads:

"Connor, best on a speedy recovery. Team, can someone jump in on Connor's section?"

**

Looking back at the CFO described by Lencioni in *The Advantage*, the one who said: "So that's probably why I'm so tight with the money."[22]

He continued. "I don't ever want to be poor like that again."[23]

As Lencioni described it, "[t]he room was silent as everyone digested the subtle magnitude of that statement.It was amazing to watch the executives immediately begin to reassess their attitudes toward the CFO, and a new level of dialogue quickly ensued about the way that they discussed expenses. That would not have happened had they not taken the time to understand one another from a basic human perspective."[24]

**

22 Ibid.

23 Ibid.

24 Ibid.

The industrial revolution and its automation, eventually, morphed into the automation of human and the criticality of information technology, and information in general, at the expense of humans.

Yet, the internet revolution is slowly showing us that even in a connected age, humans are important, and the health of employees and the health of the organization may trump information.

However, are partners of firms, subject matter experts, equipped to improve the health of their organization, which often pride themselves in the machine like nature of their associates? Maybe some are. But I think they could use some help. And can, at a minimum, improve.

**

The first step in getting better is understanding the foundations of the H4L culture. As touched on in the introduction, those foundational principles are Honesty, Inner Awareness, Removing Anxiety, Engaging Alumni, and Demonstration.

Let's take a quick look at each.

Honesty – Many if not most organizations are dysfunctional when it comes to honesty. Employees can be dishonest about their goals, plans, and desires; and management can be dishonest about employees' long-term prospects, what employees need to advance, and management's own goals, plans, and desires. Creating a safe and vulnerable environment that accepts imperfection can create win-win situations for organizations, managers, and employees.

Inner Awareness – Could very well be re-titled— "Honesty with ourselves." Young professionals, whether it's from ego, or necessity driven by the up-or-out system many firms employ, must learn to better evaluate themselves so that they can make better decisions when options are available. And so that they can better understand where they need to improve, and accept where they need to improve, which becomes critical in the execution of H4L.

Removing Anxiety – Firms can be heavily prestige based. Relative prestige is constantly tracked and monitored, relative prestige of feeder schools are constantly tracked and monitored and some combination of those two factors for a given associate make up a significant percentage of one's impression of that associate. A lack of inner awareness can create significant status anxiety about one's place in the industry. By removing this anxiety, young professionals can make decisions based on what is best for them, rather than what will improve their status.

Engaging Alumni – Alumni has the potential to be such a powerful tool for firms. Some embrace it, some do not. Those that embrace their Alumni network sow the seeds for a constant stream of work referrals ($$), employee referrals ($$), and enhanced reputations which can lead to both work and employee referrals ($$$$).

Demonstration – H4L asks for honesty, for inner awareness, for removing anxiety and dropping the focus on status and prestige, and for engaging alumni to help new alumni, and build the firm's network. For employees to be vulnerable, and buy into the H4L foundational principles, they must trust that the organization and management will hold up their end of the bargain. Organizations can ensure this trust through demonstration. For example, demonstrating that when an employee is honest, they don't get burned.

Part II of this book will take a deep dive into each of these foundational principles.

Key Takeaways on The New Landscape:

- H4L works best when the Organizational Culture, Management, and Employees buy in.
- But there can still be some level of benefit if at least two of the three groups buy in.
- Change will start by getting to know each other better.

CHAPTER 2

TODAY'S EMPLOYEES

Let's meet Abtin Buergari.

Just about everything you need to know about Buergari is nicely summed up by the title of Julie Bort's 2014 Business Insider profile of him: "This Guy Was Fired And Sued By His Employer, So He Launched A Startup And Got Sweet Revenge."[25]

Buergari was working as a paralegal for an electronic discovery company that helped law firms and other organizations with their litigation discovery needs.

25 Bort, Julie. 2014. "This Guy Was Fired And Sued By His Employer, So He Launched A Startup And Got Sweet Revenge". *Business Insider*. https://www.businessinsider.com/modus-ceo-from-jobless-to-success-2014-4.

As Bort described it, "[A] customer, an attorney, requested Buergari uncover documents as quickly and as cost-effectively as possible. Buergari had some ideas for using technology to sift through documents faster and cheaper and asked his bosses if he could try those ideas."[26]

As will be discussed extensively later, what Buergari was doing is what is referred to as Job Crafting, which is simply changing at least some portion of one's job to pursue a new way of thinking, something more interesting, a curiosity, and so forth. Bort goes on to describe how Buergari's company reacted to his initiative.

"They shushed him."[27]

Now, this is not surprising. It's not surprising because in any aspect of legal practice, whether a firm or service provider, work is typically billed hourly. Therefore, an employee wanting to experiment on the clock isn't exactly the best way to utilize that employee's time.

There is a perception among associates, that if you tell a partner about a great idea you have, you're most likely to be met with this conversation:

---

26 Ibid.
27 Ibid.

"Mr. Partner, I have a great idea for [really anything]."

"Is it billable?"

"No. But it *might* help us bill more hours later."

"Go bill."

So I understand them telling Buergari "no." Only that's not why he sees them as telling him "no."

According to Bort's article,"[T]hat's because eDiscovery is expensive for lawyers and lucrative for those supplying the document review services. The average legal department spends about $3 million per case for the discovery portion, *law blog ABA Journal* reports. They didn't want their eDiscovery process to become faster and cheaper, Buergari says."[28]

He even offered to "quit his job and become a consultant for his employer and tried to get them to let him try his ideas that way."[29]

Seems like a reasonable plan. Right? Nope. They sued him instead.

---

28 Ibid.

29 Ibid.

"I was not only fired, I was also sued." He said. His employer accused him of trying to steal their clients and their trade secrets.[30]

Plan B for Buergari then.

"He created his own eDiscovery software and cloud-computing service where companies can store documents that need to be reviewed, a service he calls 'hosted review.'"[31]

Nice! How'd it turn out?

According to Bolt, "[In 2013], Modus was named on the Inc. 5000 list of fastest-growing companies with $18 million in sales, up from $7.5 million the year before. He raised $10 million in venture funds that year, too."[32]

Not bad for a 'millennial' who also happened to be fired and sued at his last job.

**

Discussion of today's workforce has been dominated by "how to deal with millennials." This makes sense, with

---

30 Ibid.

31 Ibid.

32 Ibid.

the Millennial generation stretching to as late as the late '90s, the tail end of this generation is in college or is new to the workforce, and for those on the older side, starting a second (or third) career, possibly graduate school.

In her 2017 BBC article, Amanda Ruggeri sums up millennials beautifully:

"I know the ultimate millennial. She owns a bicycle in lieu of a car, goes to yoga class at least twice a week, grows her own bean sprouts and works side-gigs instead of for a full-time employer – she left a budding career as an economist to pursue her dream of being a comedian."[33]

That about sums it up for me! Oh wait, Ruggeri continues.

"The problem is she's not a millennial. She's a baby boomer in her late 50s."[34]

In fact, Ruggeri's conclusion is succinct:

"So basically, millennials are the same as other generations were at their age. Only a little different. More global, maybe.

---

33 Ruggeri, Amanda. 2017. "What Everyone Gets Wrong About 'Millennial Snowflakes'". *Bbc.Com.* http://www.bbc.com/capital/story/20171003-millennials-are-the-generation-thats-fun-to-hate.

34 Ibid.

More diverse. More progressive. Definitely poorer. But a unique group of monsters, the entitled wrath of which the world has ever seen before? I'm not so sure. But I'll get back to you after I've taken a few more selfies."[35]

**

In other words, other than continuing trends that have been advancing through many generations, and having some quirks related to a once-in-lifetime recession, millennials are pretty much the same as anyone else.

But what about the workforce in general then? What do workers, including millennials, want?

I think they want at least two things:

1. Flexibility in what they do, when they do it, and in using that flexibility to make in impact (either at work or in the world); and
2. Training and experience necessary to advance their career, at their either current job or elsewhere.

**

---

35 Ibid.

FLEXIBILITY

Buergari, was looking to job craft, looking for some flexibility, could also be classified as a "Millennial." Those millennials, always off, thinking of crazy things to do except work.

Well, let's look at another "not bad." Let's also use this as an opportunity to put in perspective the similarities between millennials and older generations. Specifically, let's meet John Lasseter as profiled by *The Alliance.* Lasseter was born in the 1950s. So *not* a Millennial.

"Lasseter began his career at Disney as a young animation designer in the days when animation was created with pen and paper, then converted into film. One day, a colleague showed him a video from a local conference about the emerging technology of computer-generated animation.

"Lasseter was struck by a vision. Disney should create an entire film using computer-generated animation. He went to the managers and pitched the idea. They listened carefully to his pitch; then sent him back to his desk. A few minutes later, he received a phone call from the head of Disney's animation department — informing him that he was being fired."[36]

36 Hoffman, Reid, Chris Yeh, and Ben Casnocha. 2013. *The Alliance.* London: HarperCollins.

Despite the disparate fields, one a service provider to a service firm, the other a Hollywood goliath, both companies had the same reaction to a young employee bringing a new idea. Specifically, an idea that could change the financial dynamic of the company—fire them.

Why was he fired? "[H]e was too distracted with his crazy ideas."[37]

But I'll be honest, this rationale doesn't ring true to me. I suspect Lasseter didn't buy it either. Think about why Buergari was fired. If he succeeded, he would have greatly reduced the amount of time (read "dollars") that his company made. And they didn't have the vision to understand how to monetize the new proposed service.

Lasseter's idea would also have had a dramatic effect on the feature-film animation business. Whereas, before you had countless artists hand drawing individual frames of a film, now you would have, presumably fewer artists (who were also computer animators, rather than traditional artists) making movies in potentially less time.

Thankfully, that was not the end of Lasseter's story. You probably already know it.

---

37 Ibid.

"He joined George Lucas's Lucasfilm, where he pursued computer animation as a member of Ed Catmull's computer division. A few years later, Lucas sold the then-unprofitable division to Steve Jobs, who named the resulting company Pixar."[38]

Whoops.

This mistake "Would cost them. The Walt Disney Company spent over $7 billion to buy Pixar. And that's how Lasseter ended up back at Disney as its Chief Creative Officer of Disney Animation Studios."[39]

If you remember from Chapter 1, I talked about whether we should be treating associates like fungible resources. *The Alliance* uses similar terminology with respect to Lasseter: "Commodity."

Specifically, "Disney's management hired an entrepreneurial talent like Lasseter, but they treated him as a commodity rather than an ally. And in the process, they lost their chance to develop a multibillion-dollar business. Lasseter would have been happy to develop that business within Disney, but his managers wouldn't let him."[40]

---

38 Ibid.

39 Ibid.

40 Ibid.

**

TRAINING

While Buergari and Lasseter were looking for flexibility to charge after a new idea, most, if not all, are looking to get better at what they do. They are looking for training.

The 2018 Deloitte Millennial Survey was telling with respect to what Millennials and Gen Z expect from their employers.

"Millennials credit school or university studies with 23 percent of the skills, knowledge, and experience they currently have or use in their jobs; among Gen Z, only a few years after graduation, the figure is still only 26 percent. On-the-job training from employers or from continuous professional development carries much more weight: In combination, these two sources are estimated to contribute 52 percent of what millennials draw on at work (44 percent for Gen Z)."[41]

In other words, of the total skills the younger workforce needs, they think about half will come from on the job training and formal work provided training. Yet, only about a quarter from schooling.

---

41 "Deloitte Global Millennial Survey 2018". 2018. *Deloitte*. https://www2.deloitte.com/global/en/pages/about-deloitte/articles/millennialsurvey.html.

Anyone who has gone to a professional school knows this tracks with reality. There is only so much you can learn in school.

But this tends to create a vicious cycle. If you remember back in Chapter 1 the conversation the associate Sam had with the partner about getting upset with,"Training a professional only to have them leave and compete." You realize this is inevitable. It has to be.

If a person can only learn 25% of what they need to learn at school, they have to get the rest elsewhere. *Someone* has to teach them.

The Alliance **nails** this concept. Just accept they might leave. Make an ethical agreement with them that you'll train them if they stay.

Sir Richard Branson is quoted as saying, "Train people well enough that they can leave, treat them well enough so they don't want to."

"Employer training and support quite obviously help millennials and the Gen Z cohort perform their jobs, and as their careers progress, the role of employer as educator will take on even greater significance. The concept of businesses as educators has been gaining traction, and this year's survey results clearly substantiate its value: 73 percent of those who plan to stay with their employers more than five years say their organizations are strong providers of education and training."[42]

**

In Chapter 1, we touched on what the new landscape for Culture-Management-Employee relationships could look like, and how the foundations of H4L will build that landscape.

The next step will be better understanding how to execute H4L. Those more tactical execution principles are: Career Conversations; Performance Conversations; The Playbook; Job Crafting; and The Long Game.

Let's take a quick look at each.

Career Conversations – Career conversations are conversations between employees and management about how an employee's career aspirations can help an organization, and about how the organization can help an employee realize those goals. When employees and management have honest careers conversations, then both sides can tailor the experience to maximize benefit to all parties.

42 Ibid.

Performance Conversations – Unlike career conversations, performance conversations detail the *execution* of an employee's career goals. Performance conversations focus on *actionable* feedback, both positive and growth, to ensure that an employee stays on path to reach their career goals, and to ensure that management is holding up their end of the bargain.

The Playbook – Firms are unique from traditional organizations in that it is very common for associates to work with multiple senior employees. The Playbook is a way to give new associates "cheat sheets" into various senior employees to help them hit the ground running.

Job Crafting – As touched on above, Job Crafting is a system where employees are given agency of some portion of their job duties. This could allow employees to focus on a particular type of work they like (reasonably common already in many firms); can allow employees to test other practice areas to explore a practice area change (reasonably uncommon); can allow entrepreneurial employees to chart their own course – for example a junior associate building business early, or an associate exploring new ways for the firm to make money (both reasonably uncommon).

The Long Game – All roads lead here. Firms' existence can span decades, generations, centuries; and employees' careers can span 40+ years. Rather than being shortsighted, organizations, management, and employees should consider how each group can impact the value of each other group well beyond the initial relationship end.

Part IV of this book will take a deep dive into each of these execution principles.

**

Key Takeaways on Today's Employees:

- Except for some long-term changes in a small subset of characteristics that have been happening for multiple generations, Millennials and Gen Z workers have a lot in common with previous generations of workers.
- Workers want flexibility in what they do, when they do it, and in using that flexibility to make in impact (either at work or in the world).
- Workers are looking for training and experience necessary to advance their career, at either their current job or elsewhere.

PART II

THE H4L FOUNDATION

CHAPTER 3

HONESTY

"Many HR leaders and executives get frustrated when they spend a lot of money on training and development programs, only to see employees walk out the door months later. If you think of your employees as free agents, the natural response is to slash training budgets. Why train a competitor's new hire? In an alliance, the manager can speak openly and honestly about the investment the company is willing to make in the employee and what it expects in return. The employee can speak openly and honestly about the type of growth he seeks (skills, experiences, and the like) and what he will invest in the company in return by way of effort and commitment. Both sides set clear expectations."[43]

43 Hoffman, Reid, Chris Yeh, and Ben Casnocha. 2013. *The Alliance*. London: HarperCollins.

That's again from *The Alliance*. The clearest example discussed in *The Alliance* about the power of honesty, specifically long-term career honesty, is the story of Matt Cohler.

As told in *The Alliance*, "Cohler left the high pay and brand umbrella of McKinsey & Company to join LinkedIn, then a tiny start-up that was living in the shadow of Friendster." This is a familiar path so many firm associates follow— work for the firm for a number of years, and then move in-house. In this case, a startup.[44]

But this is where things were different. "Reid [Hoffman], as CEO, was his new boss and did something none of Cohler's previous managers had done. Rather than simply hiring Cohler into a particular job or position, Reid worked with the young consultant to define an explicit tour of duty that would help both employer and employee."[45]

In other words, Hoffman offered to be honest with Cohler, if Cohler would agree to be honest with him in return.

"Cohler's goal was to become a venture capitalist."[46]

44 Ibid.
45 Ibid.
46 Ibid.

I'm thinking of the courage it would take to tell someone early in a job that you had long-term aspirations to have a different job, even when that person tells you to be honest with them about your goals. I had that courage once, but back to Cohler.

Not only was Reid not fazed by this honesty, but also he fought to "keep" Cohler and worked to convince him that his current job could be refined to help him with his long-term goals.

As *The Alliance* explains, "Reid argued that gaining operational experience at a successful start-up was a better path to being named a general partner at a venture capital firm than trying to join a firm straight out of McKinsey. Reid pitched Cohler on a unique tour of duty. Cohler would act as Reid's right-hand person. In this role, he would learn from the company's CEO and get extremely broad exposure to all the functional areas in the business."[47]

That's quite an offer.

Not only did Cohler get the usual job perks, but he also got a job description custom made to reach his post LinkedIn goals. But such offers don't come for free. And it's important

---

47 Ibid.

to note that while I will discuss where customizing aspects of some jobs can result in fewer total hours of work — H4L is not about employees having easy jobs.

Not only do I not believe that the job Cohler got was easy, but I imagine it was extremely demanding. As *The Alliance* describes it: "[I]n exchange, Cohler committed to doing whatever it took to build the business, regardless of whether those projects fell under any traditional job titles or career paths. By completing this mission, Cohler would add both the LinkedIn and Reid Hoffman brands to his personal portfolio. Thus, even though Cohler's ultimate goal of becoming a venture capitalist necessarily lay beyond LinkedIn's boundaries, he and Reid were able to align their short-term aspirations and interests."[48]

**

"A 2010 study by the Corporate Executive Board found that companies that encouraged honest feedback among its staff, and that rated highly in the area of open communication, delivered a 10-year total shareholder return that was 270 percent more than other companies—7.9 percent compared to 2.1 percent. That's impressive."[49]

---

48 Ibid.

49 Westfall, Brian. 2019. "Why Honesty Is The Secret Ingredient Of Successful Organizations". Software Advice. Accessed June 30.

It's not surprising honesty matters — it's a lot like saying we like baseball and apple pie.

But honesty implies something entirely transformational in a H4L relationship.

Honesty and transparency are foundational in framing the relationship of a new employee within the context of the traditional partnership model. H4L relationships aren't built on the "wink, wink, nod, nod" communication style that you aren't *really* going to be a partner some day; H4L relationships are explicit:

Odds are you won't make partner here; but you'll be setup for an incredible career *after* you're here regardless.

**

I mentioned that I had, as in "used to have" the courage to have an honest conversations about career goals with management. That's why Cohler's story strikes such a nerve with me.

Hearing his story brought me back to a job I had prior to my legal career. I was an engineer with a defense-contracting

---

https://www.softwareadvice.com/resources/why-honesty-is-the-secret-ingredient-of-successful-organizations/.

firm. Prior to taking the job, I was already in the process of studying for the Law School Admission Test, I was open with my future boss, who we'll call Steve, during the interview process, and even asked for time during my first couple weeks of work to study for and take the LSAT. I was offered, and accepted, the job, and was granted the "free time." In fact, Steve wrote me a letter of recommendation for admission to law school. Yet, things still didn't work out.

I can say with no guilty conscious that I took this job with good intentions. I fully expected to stay throughout law school and beyond. My plan was to study project management during the day at work, and eventually get my Project Management Professional (PMP) certificate. And to go to law school at night. In my head, I was getting a JD + (Real-World) MBA. If I was determined to get an attorney job, then I would focus on internal jobs first.

Stepping back, I am a sucker for motivational speeches. Especially, when they align with what I want in my head. For every lunch where I complained about the injustices that were taking place at the law firm and how the path to partnership was a lie, there was another time where I would walk out of a meeting about the path to partnership thinking:

"You know what, I think I can make partner!"

Things were going well at this job. I was performing well and getting good recognition. The first bump in the road happened when I told them I was accepted into law school. Yet, they knew right? Yes, they did know. Regardless, school would prevent me from traveling, and the project I was currently on required significant travel. Despite my initial honestly, this change still rubbed some people the wrong way.

While I thought I was being honest, it's still always important to look at what I could have done better as well. As an example, maybe I should have been very clear upfront that law school would mean no traveling.

In any event, I was moved to another project that needed someone with my skill set, and they found someone to replace me. In other words, everyone was good.

I began to actively seek new work to build up my credentials for the PMP certificate, which requires a certain number of hours as an actual project manager. I reached out to Steve about getting a small project to manage. He told me he had a perfect project that related to some kind of widget that needed to be delivered. This was exciting for me. I had just been accepted to law school and now I was getting my own project to manage.

Things were looking pretty good for my law school at night, business school during the day plan.

Then came "The speech."

This firm, like many, had trouble with retention. The reason, as it was explained to me, had to do with the nature of government contracts, which made it necessary for workers to job hop to get anything other than a cost of living raise. A senior member of our division of the firm, who we'll call Dave, called a meeting to address attrition. To say that I was genuinely moved by his speech would be an understatement. I was psyched! It went something like this:

"We need to be a stronger community!"

"We shouldn't let preconceived notions about money cause us to lose people."

"We need to be able to talk with each other more, have lunch together . . . build relationships."

"Most importantly, if you are thinking about leaving, or if you are unhappy, or want to do something different, you need to let us know, you need to let ME know."

"I'll have a one-on-one with anyone who wants to sit and chat about their career here."

I was on his calendar that same day for a meeting the following week.

The meeting went even better than expected. There was talk about how the legal skill set could be helpful in the firm context and how the firm employed many lawyers. So I could look into that to stay with the company, and how he was glad that his talk resonated with me and that I scheduled the time to talk with him. I talked to him about how Steve was lining me up for my first project to manage, and Dave agreed that I was on the right path.

"Wow," I thought, "this being honest with management is great!"

Why did I have the courage to have this conversation with Dave? I felt safe from danger.

**

"The world was filled with danger. All of these forces are working very, very hard to kill us. Nothing personal."[50]

---

50 "Why Good Leaders Make You Feel Safe | Simon Sinek". 2019. *Youtube*. https://www.youtube.com/watch?v=lmyZMtPVodo.

That's from Simon Sinek's TED talk "Why good leaders make you feel safe." There he's describing human existence 50,000 years ago. But things haven't changed much. Sure, the physical dangers are greatly reduced, also not particularly relevant to this book, but the concept holds remarkably true, unfortunately, in the workplace. Replace World with Workplace and Kill with Fire and you pretty much nail a good portion of organizations' environments.

Sinek put it more eloquently: "The world is filled with danger, things [are] trying to frustrate our lives or reduce our success, reduce our opportunity for success."[51]

"Trust and cooperation are really important here. The problem with the concepts of trust in cooperation is that they are feelings. They are not instructions. I can't simply say to you 'trust me,' and you will. I can't simply instruct two people to cooperate, and they will."[52]

Our reaction 50,000 years ago, as Sinek tells us was evolve "Into social animals, where we lived together and worked together in what I call a circle of safety, inside the tribe, where we felt like we belonged. And when we felt safe amongst our own, the natural reaction was trust and cooperation. There

51 Ibid.
52 Ibid.

are inherent benefits to this. It means I can fall asleep at night and trust that someone from within my tribe will watch for danger. If we don't trust each other, if I don't trust you that means you won't watch for danger."[53]

Trust. Cooperation. Safety.

**

But safety alone does not create sufficient trust to cooperate with management and be honest.

In her TED Talk "The Power of Vulnerability" Brené Brown describes how her research into shame led to learning the power of vulnerability. Specifically, she talks about how she focused her analysis on those she studied who had a strong sense of love and belonging. She wanted to see what these people had in common.[54]

First, "They had a sense of courage." Brown distinguished courage from bravery here. "Courage, the original definition of courage, when it first came into the English language—it's from the Latin word "cor," meaning "heart"—and the original definition was to tell the story of who you are with your

53 Ibid.

54 "The Power Of Vulnerability | Brené Brown". 2019. *Youtube.* https://www.youtube.com/watch?v=iCvmsMzlF7o.

whole heart. And so these folks had, very simply, the courage to be imperfect."[55]

**

The courage to be imperfect.

Before we learn more from Brown about vulnerability, I think it is critical we take a look at this last statement about accepting imperfection. Not only does it appear to be critical to vulnerability, and therefore, in my opinion, critical to honesty, it is also critical to being open to growth.

In *Mindset*, Carol Dweck discusses how those with a growth mindset have a similar courage to be imperfect.

"[S]tudies show that people are terrible at estimating their abilities."[56]

Ouch.

Dweck and her team looked into this. They found that while "People greatly misestimated their performance and their ability, those with the fixed mindset . . . accounted for almost

55 Ibid.

56 Dweck, Carol. 2016. *Mindset*. New York: Random House.

all the inaccuracy. The people with the growth mindset were amazingly accurate."[57]

Digging deeper: "[W]hen you think about it, this makes sense. If, like those with the growth mindset, you believe you can develop yourself, then you're open to accurate information about your current abilities, even if it's unflattering. What's more, if you're oriented toward learning, as they are, you need accurate information about your current abilities in order to learn effectively."[58]

The courage to be imperfect and the necessity to have a greater inner awareness will be addressed more fully in the next chapter.

**

Back to Brown, the second thing that the people in her focused analysis had in common was "[T]hey fully embraced vulnerability. They didn't talk about vulnerability being comfortable, nor did they really talk about it being excruciating. They just talked about it being necessary. They talked about the willingness to do something where there are no guarantees. They're willing to invest in

57 Ibid.
58 Ibid.

a relationship that may or may not work out. They thought this was fundamental."[59]

Trust. Cooperation. Safety. Vulnerability. Courage. Honesty.

Hoffman had the courage to make such an offer to Cohler, and Cohler had the courage to be honest with Hoffman about what his goals were. Hoffman and Cohler were both vulnerable to the notion that this might not work out. They were willing to accept those consequences, and because these characteristics were all present in the relationship between Hoffman and Cohler, early signs pointed to that relationship being mutually beneficial. A win-win.

That was where I thought things were headed for me, as well, after my conversation with Dave about my own career goals.

**

I genuinely don't remember when the next part of my story happened, but it was, at most, a couple of weeks. I asked Steve about the status of the widget project, and he told me that we were a couple of weeks out from getting that started. As I said, my meeting with Dave was amazing. What's another couple weeks to wait?

59 "The Power Of Vulnerability | Brené Brown". 2019. *Youtube*. https://www.youtube.com/watch?v=iCvmsMzlF7o.

Within a couple of days of that conversation, I was sitting at my desk when a friend in the cube next to me got a call. Due to the nature of a cube farm, it was hard to avoid unintentionally eavesdropping. Worse yet, although perhaps better from a comedy standpoint, I was only getting one side of the conversation. It went something like this:

"Hi this is John . . . Yeah, I'd love get a small project to manage. What's it related to? . . . Widget delivery . . . Cool . . ."

I'm sure you see where this is going.

I popped over to his cube.

"Hi John, couldn't help but overhear the conversation you just had. But I'm concerned that it sounded like you were being asked to manage a project that sounded suspiciously like the one I was asked to manage."

"No clue dude. Steve just called and asked if I would be interested."

I walked directly into Steve's office and explained what I had overheard. He confessed that he had been ordered by Dave to take the project away from me. Dave said to him: "He's just gonna quit as soon as he graduates from law school."

So what went wrong?

If you remember back in Chapter 1, I talked about how H4L requires at least two, and ideally all three, of Culture, Manager, and Employee. My situation at the defense contractor has only one, Employee (yours truly). Dave, representing Culture (organization president) not only didn't believe in H4L principles, but worse presented himself as following those principles. And Steve, in the Manager role, wasn't in a position to effect change.

**

So now, we know what happened to me. But whatever happened to Cohler? Cohler trusted Hoffman. Hoffman gave Cohler a similar speech to what Dave gave to me. And Cohler opened up to Hoffman just like I opened up to Dave. Let's return to *The Alliance.*

Cohler's story continues at another social network. "After three years at LinkedIn, Cohler approached [Hoffman] to tell him that he was thinking about leaving LinkedIn to join an even younger social networking start-up that called itself 'The Facebook.'" This is interesting for a number of reasons to me. First, Cohler's not leaving LinkedIn for his goal, but for another tech company. Second, while Facebook and

LinkedIn were not direct competitors, they, at a minimum, had to compete for attention and advertising.[60]

Regardless, Hoffman kept Cohler's best interest in mind. Specifically, "He advised Cohler to accept the Facebook offer, since it would help him move closer to his goal of becoming a venture capitalist by giving him greater diversity of start-up experience."[61]

Hoffman's guidance proved to be exactly what Cohler needed to reach his dream. As told in *The Alliance* "[A]fter four years at Facebook, Cohler left for a new tour of duty—this time as a general partner at Benchmark, one of Silicon Valley's top venture firms."[62]

Win-Win situations are not necessarily about maximizing the value added to one party or the other. But rather about making sure both parties gain sufficient value to make the relationship worth it. Cohler's relationship with LinkedIn and Hoffman is a clear win-win. Both during Cohler's employment at LinkedIn and helping him achieve his career goal.

---

60 Hoffman, Reid, Chris Yeh, and Ben Casnocha. 2013. *The Alliance.* London: HarperCollins.

61 Ibid.

62 Ibid.

But it doesn't stop there. Further, as we'll see, this is the true power of H4L. Cohler performed critical tasks for LinkedIn as an employee, and was rewarded with experience and his dream job. But his value back to LinkedIn continues.

"[Hoffman] has Cohler speak with high-value LinkedIn employees to explain the benefits of undertaking a tour of duty at the company. Reid and Matt Cohler still have a close relationship; for example, they sit together on the board of Edmodo, a start-up they invested in together in 2011. Matt Cohler's tour of duty at LinkedIn presents a textbook case of a mutually beneficial alliance that persists even after the official employment relationship has ended."[63]

**

Years later, I went into an annual review and got a pretty typical review:

"We love working with you. You do great work. Best year you've had here. Big improvements in hours and efficiency but both could always be improved."

I got a bonus and promotion. However, one of the partners also hit me with this:

63 Ibid.

"Listen Chris, you're doing great, but are you happy with the job? Are you even interested with pushing for partner here? If you are thinking you might like something else, maybe in-house, let us know. We can help place you."

I particularly liked his closing line:

"Maybe you wake up every morning, lay there in bed, and think 'there's literally anywhere I would rather go this morning than the firm.'"

This was a very generous and thoughtful offer. And that partner should be commended for making it. And I was thinking that maybe in-house was my long-term plan. This was potentially just the opportunity that I was looking for.

Alas, I told them exactly what I had been conditioned to tell them, which was that I wanted to be a partner at that firm, but if something changed, I appreciated the offer and would let them know.

Much of this was my baggage, but there also wasn't a foundation of trust built by the firm to me either. I hadn't observed anything that demonstrated that I should trust them.

**

Honesty is critical to H4L, and trust, along with related principles of safety, courage, and vulnerability, are critical to honest communications.

Trust has two overarching elements when we interact with others: First, do you trust a person to perform an action – complete a task or care for someone or something; Second, do you trust a person with your information?

Honesty impacts, and is impacted by, both.

Most relevant to my story, because I didn't trust the partners with my information, I was reluctant to honestly communicate my career goals.

It isn't hard to imagine how things could have worked out if I was honest with the partners, and if they were honest with their offer. We already know how Matt Cohler's story ended. But again, what about me?

What very likely could have happened is that, just like in Cohler's case, everyone could have won. There is no reason that I couldn't have worked at the firm for the same amount of time that I did. But if I had been honest, and if the firm had returned that honesty, I could have been placed at a firm client. I would have been thrilled to leave on ideal terms and the firm could have reaffirmed a client commitment to the firm with me.

**

Key Takeaways:

- Honesty is enabled when people have the courage to be imperfect and are vulnerable in a safe environment that engenders trust and coordination.
- Honesty is foundational to the H4L environment. A corporate culture of honesty. Management who are honest with Employees. Employees who are honest with Management, and themselves.
- Honest environments allow win-win scenarios between organizations and their employees.

CHAPTER 4

INNER AWARENESS

"I understood that I sucked."[64]

I'll never forget hearing that line for the first time. It genuinely floored me.

I heard it on a radio interview recently that involved two of my favorite people, Howard Stern and Chris Rock, and the conversation was fascinating. In Stern, you have a radio personality who has defied his critics and endured for almost 40 years, throughout that time graduating from shock antics to hours-long interviews with living legends. He's also a man with a truly world class ego. While loved by critics sooner

64 Rock, Chris. 2014. The Howard Stern Show. Interview by Howard Stern. Radio. Sirius XM. Radio.

in his career, Rock similarly has endured and seemingly only improved.

What struck me about this particular conversation was, despite their egos, I'd argue, their justified egos, both have incredibly similar early careers with a high level of self awareness. Both, considered top of their field, both knew that they weren't ready for the big time yet, and played small clubs, or small market radio stations to hone their craft. This shows a level of patience rare among your typical elite prospect.

Rock would watch other comedians succeed, and he was okay with their success because in his mind, he knew they were better than he.

Saying "I didn't get frustrated until there came a point where I said, 'Okay, I'm better than this famous guy. I should be up here right now.'"[65]

Yes, there was a point where he perceived his own skill to outstrip those around him that were succeeding. And that moment of perception likely triggered a choice on his part to take a step up. However, until that time, and I'm sure after that time while he was at the next level, he was realistic with his ability.

65 Ibid.

Rock says, "I kind of accepted my plight, like you did. A lot of guys don't accept their plight. They are unrealistic with where their talent is. And it's like 'Dude, you're not that good right now. That's what we have in common. I understood that I sucked."[66]

**

So many people, and it's hard to fault them for this, routinely take the path that would result in a promotion, more money, or an objectively better resume.

With respect to their careers, both Stern and Rock have a growth mindset.

How does Howard Stern know he needs to stay longer in Hartford? How does Chris Rock know he needs to continue to tour small clubs?

Further to our discussion of *Mindset* in Chapter 3, Dweck also cites to Howard Gardner. Who identifies this self-analysis as almost like a skill. "[I]n his book *Extraordinary Minds*, [Gardner] concluded that exceptional individuals

66 Ibid.

have 'a special talent for identifying their own strengths and weaknesses.'"[67]

Dweck astutely notes that "[i]t's interesting that those with the growth mindset seem to have that talent."[68]

**

Assessing one's current skill level, whether it makes sense to take a promotion or whether a resume building job makes sense, is a problem that plagues the modern professional services firm model, both from the firm perspective and the associate perspective.

We all know about up-or-out. Associates face the very possibility that, if they aren't ready for promotion, they could potentially lose their job.

Firms want associates to move up to maximize profit (very understandable) or out to make room for a potentially higher performing associate. Associates want to move up to be paid more and pay off those crushing student loans.

---

67 Dweck, Carol. 2016. *Mindset*. New York: Random House.
68 Ibid.

It doesn't, however, always make sense for a firm to force an underperforming associate out. First, there is no guarantee that a replacement associate would actually perform better. And, second, they've just spent time and money training the associate, and the real associate profits start to roll in after the first couple of years.

All of these things can combine to result in an associate being in a class year with a billing rate out of whack with that associate's ability.

Here how this could look:

- Fee for project type of $3000
- Associate billing at $300/hour
- Associate improve from 15 hours to 10 hours for project type
- At the beginning of the year, associate is billing $4500 for a $3000 project
- At end of a year, associate is billing $3000 for a $3000 project
- Fee for the project type still $3000
- Associate now billing at $400/hour
- Associate improves from 10 hours to 8 hours for a project type
- Just after promotion, associate is billing $4000 for a $3000 project

- At the end of the year, associate is billing $3200 for a $3000 project

**

This is exactly what happened to Glen.

At the time, Glen was a junior associate at a big firm.

"I had just finished my first full year. I made my hours, although barely, and while I knew I needed to work on my efficiency, I thought I did well enough and was improving. Because I hit that magical hours mark, and got at least a passing review, I was even awarded a full market bonus!

"I guess I just assumed that was the end of it."

But it wasn't. As Glen soon found out.

After handing him his check, the partner said "Glen, we think you're really improving. We're happy with the trend line for hours and efficiency. But . . ."

Glen didn't need to take a negotiations class to know that in this case "but" was a bad thing.

As the partner explained to him, "But, we don't think that you are going to be able to support a higher billing rate yet."

As Glen told me, "I didn't know what was happening. I always just assumed that if you couldn't support a higher billing rate, you were out. So I was starting to prepare myself to be let go."

The partner continued, "We don't think it makes sense to advance your class at this time. We think it will be really helpful for you long term to have another year to improve your efficiency, and then be ready to advance next year."

The good news was that Glen was not fired, but that didn't mean that it didn't impact him.

"Needless to say, I was shocked when I was told that I was not going to advance a class year. This was a huge blow to me.

"My biggest concern was what it meant for my career. Was this really "helping" my partnership chances as I was told? I didn't buy it. These partners are cratering my career unfairly, I thought, and giving me a line so they can keep me around until they recoup their investment. What are the other partners going to think when they see an associate was held back? My partnership chances are dead."

Glen is not alone in thinking this way, but it is the wrong way of thinking. Whether a firm is globally, nationally, or regionally elite, they are hiring associates who are coming from elite law schools, or who were elite at their regional law school. These associates, like star athletes, are accustomed to moving up, to keep pace with their peers, to succeed.

Every year there are countless star college football players who go undrafted, players drafted in lower than expected rounds, and drafted players who don't start.

An elite professional prospect faces the same reality. A top degree with honors from a top law school does not guarantee partnership. It doesn't even guarantee a job much less an annual promotion at an elite firm. A class demotion is often just too much for the associate ego to handle. In the associate's mind, it's much better to just lateral to another firm, and buy yourself a couple more years at higher pay.

**

With respect to inner awareness, we've so far been talking about awareness of one's ability at a given point in time. There is, however, another type of inner awareness that is equally and critically important:

Is the role you are in the right role for you?

If you know a role is wrong, this can be handled a couple different ways, including: job crafting and quitting.

But first, you have to determine whether a role is right for you.

This is something my friend Paul went through.

Paul was an ex-attorney who worked at a firm in a non-lawyer role. Paul and I hung out a lot and maintained our friendship beyond our respective firms. But despite our many conversations and me knowing that he started his career as a lawyer, I never really knew why he switched to a non-legal route. Or the thought process that he went through to get to that point, other than the typical bill-a-lot-of-hours burnout.

And the reality was that hours and burnout were a huge component, but there was so much more. Paul actually showed a tremendous amount of inner awareness. He was honest with himself.

When we recently spoke, he told me what he was thinking.

"For me, I was thinking 'this is pretty brutal.'"

Not an uncommon refrain from a law firm associate.

"I'm not even here two years. For me to make it to a point where maybe I have more control, and don't have to be doing the kind of work I'm doing is like six years of running the gauntlet. And I just do not have it in me."

This is a hard thing to say. But inner awareness is not the only game in town. Others have their opinions as well. And status anxiety (deep dive in the next chapter) is not just an inner awareness issue.

Paul's father had the following reaction:

"You what?! Three years in school and you're only one-and-a-half years at a firm and you already want to quit?"

As Paul said, and as you can imagine, "It did not go over well."

Some of the other push back he got, I imagine from not only family and friends, but also the firm itself when he quit were typical:

"Why are you quitting?"

"Why are you giving up?"

These are the kinds of things that are said on a regular basis, and some of them make sense, especially from a quick economic reaction standpoint: you spent three years and $X to become a lawyer, you should at least be a lawyer long enough to make that all make sense.

I guess?

So often living in misery here is just throwing good money after bad. At a minimum, it presupposes that you can't have an alternative career, which is wrong. Paul quickly got a non-legal job at a firm (which valued his prior legal experience), and then stayed there for 15 years before starting a thriving independent business, which he runs from his beach house.

It's starting to sound like he made a good choice that worked out just fine.

**

Like many associates, I went through this same conversation in my head. Like so many, I thought I wanted to be partner at big firm. And I'm sure my wife wanted me to make partner. Even beyond the money and prestige, in many ways it represents the peak of the profession. In other words, the goal of going to law school is to become a big firm partner.

But was I willing to do what is necessary to be a big firm partner? Was my wife willing to put up with what comes with that?

"Why not push for partner?" I'd hear. She would do her best to give me a pep talk.

Ultimately though, we both wanted me out. We had enough missed child events and busted vacations. Maybe a smaller firm would have worked, but I was just pretty sour on the idea of a firm and needed something different.

**

When I told Glen about Stern and Rock, and about inner awareness, the concepts seemed to resonate.

"I needed to be more like them," he told me, "I needed to realize that I sucked, and wasn't ready. And I needed to realize that I didn't need to be a big firm lawyer to be a success."

Glen ended up doing just fine.

"The reality is that the lower billing rate for a year was a huge relief. I did take that next year and improved my efficiency. I did end up lasting another six years at that firm.

And it might not have actually cratered my career if I had stayed longer."

Glen ended up working for a smaller firm and is on the cusp of partnership.

**

Key Takeaways:

- Many people, especially those with fixed mindsets, are bad at accurately analyzing personal performance, and identifying weakness.
- Many also struggle with realizing when they are making a career decision that is not in their best interest.
- Inner awareness, both with respect to identifying deficiencies, and being accepting of those deficiencies others identify, is critical to professional growth and making good career decisions.

CHAPTER 5

REMOVING ANXIETY

Charles was a mid-level associate a patent boutique. He had bounced around from a number of different firms, and while a close examination and thoughtful questioning might have revealed the truth, he was careful to hide the fact that he didn't choose to leave a couple of those firms.

Safely out of the law firm world now, I asked Charles what went wrong?

"I had ten years of experience on paper, and wanted to get paid like a professional with ten years of experience."

Fundamentally, that is fine. But many, if not all, professional services firms that pay associates based on years of experience, bill them out at a commensurate rate.

And you *must* be able to support that rate.

**

Taking a quick segue back to the story from Chapter 1 that Sam told me about the associate who wanted to leave to go to another firm. We'll call that associate Joan.

After talking to the Partner, and Joan, here is how Joan *first* told the partners she wanted to quit:

"I've accepted an offer at another firm."

"Why are you wanting to go to another firm, you work at a firm now? Are they giving you different work?"

"They are paying me more."

"Let's talk about that. If they are going to pay you more, they are going to demand a higher billing rate. Based on what I see, you can't support a higher billing rate."

This is a great point of course. As with Glen in Chapter 4, the firm promotes people it feels can support the promotion, whether immediately or trending in the right direction.

"I can do the work faster. I work to the rate."

The partner was stunned.

Now, I do think it's important to note that I don't think this professional was overbilling in the traditional sense, I just don't think Joan was pushing herself. This is a nuanced topic, but needless to say in this instance I think it was relatively innocent.

"Well, if you will work faster, we can pay you more. What's the offer for?"

Joan gives the number.

"At this salary, you're rate will be [some amount]. Based on that, you'd have to be able to complete this project time in 30 hours instead of 40."

"Ok, I can do that."

"Like, as soon as the salary change happens."

"No problem."

**

Back to Charles.

As discussed with Joan, a critical factor with pay at firms is your billing rate, higher the pay, higher the billing rate. And clients will only pay so much for various services. If an employee cannot support a billing rate, the situation with that employee could become unsustainable, and that employee's value to the firm may drop.

By demanding higher pay, Charles was establishing himself as someone who could support that billing rate.

I asked Charles why he accepted an offer for a job he just wasn't capable of doing.

"They actually gave me options for different billing rate and salary combinations. And I simply took the highest."

Eventually, the inevitable happened.

"I went right back to what I knew. I went looking at law firms."

Patent law is a pretty specialized field, and he was confident he would be able to get a new job at a similar pay.

"But I was starting to realize that maybe I needed to think about plan B."

Luckily, Charles has a colleague with some connection at the Patent Office, who was looking for patent examiners.

"The Patent Office felt like a step down. It felt like I would be a failure. And I knew it would be a pretty significant pay cut."

Charles was right that it was a pay cut. But it's also a government job compared to a big firm job. So sure, it is less money, but it's also less work. It's harder to get fired. Moreover, you'll get a ton of time to do your work.

Charles was convinced. He went through the process, got an offer, and was just about to accept it.

"I had the offer in hand. Then a big firm that I had applied to a month ago called. I interviewed quickly and had an offer almost right away. It met my requirement: six figures."

**

Professionals, like most adults, are constantly trying to ascertain their status relative to the status of those around them. This is a concept that author and journalist Daniel Coyle calls Status Management.

In an interview with *The Investor Guys* podcast, Coyle recounts a story about a contest designed by Peter Skillman.[69]

"The contest was really simple. Who can build the tallest tower with the following materials: twenty pieces of raw spaghetti, a yard of tape, and a single standard size marshmallow. The only rule: marshmallow has to go on the top."[70]

Coyle then tells us about the teams Skillman put together to participate in the contest. He had teams of four.

"Teams of CEOs, teams of MBAs, teams of lawyers, and teams of Kindergarteners."[71]

The initial observation was about how differently the adults (regardless of group) acted relative to the children.

"All the adult groups start out in the same way. They talk. They talk about what they are going to do. They make a plan. And they decide on ideas. And they hone those ideas. And they divvy up the roles. And they start looking. And it looks

69 Pysh, Preston, and Stig Broderson. 2019. "TIP187: The Culture Code W/ Daniel Coyle (Business Podcast)". Podcast. *We Study Billionaires – The Investor Podcast.*

70 Ibid.

71 Ibid.

gorgeous. It looks perfect. It looks very cooperative and smooth."[72]

Ah, but what about the kids?

"They just start eating a bunch of marshmallows. And it's very chaotic. And it's just – energy."[73]

You would assume that one of the adult groups would win. But, as might be obvious, they don't.

Why?

"Because our mental model of group performance is wrong. It doesn't include the two most important factors. It doesn't include status management. And it doesn't include safety."[74]

Even though the adults look organized, "they are being hindered by status management. There's a little whisper in the back of their mind. 'Where do I fit in here? Is it ok to say that? Who's in charge?' That hinders cooperation. It hinders ideation. It hinders iteration. It hinders innovation."[75]

---

72 Ibid.
73 Ibid.
74 Ibid.
75 Ibid.

But the kids think differently.

"The kindergarteners don't have any problem with that. They're not worried about status. If they see a problem, they just reach in there and fix it. There's no better feedback, than having your tower fall down."[76]

**

While status management is certainly a problem for professionals, I think the bigger problem is what I call Status Anxiety.

I view status management as how you rank yourself, and how you act relative to others in a specific context. As in Coyle's example the lawyers, the CEOs, and the MBAs size each other up to decide who will do certain tasks.

In contrast, status anxiety is the feeling that you and your career will forever be ranked and defined by your professional status, specifically where you went to school, and for what organizations you work(ed).

Back when I was considering law school, I read *How to Get Into Law School* by Susan Estrich to help me decide whether

---

76 Ibid.

law school was the right path for me. There was a lot of great information in there. But one thing that stood out then, and has only been confirmed since, is the general obsession attorney's have with prestige.

Nobody borrows credibility quite like lawyers.

It's not just what law school you went to, but where did you summer, what judge did you intern/clerk for, where were you an associate, etc. For the non-lawyers reading this, I know what you're thinking: "It's like that everywhere." I promise you it's not as bad as the legal practice. This is, in my opinion, highly related to some other unique quirks of the legal practice that will be discussed elsewhere in this book. Primarily, there is almost no way to demonstrate your legal expertise prior to actually getting an associate job.

Everyone from software developers to artists have portfolios of their work. With a developer, the program works or doesn't, and for artists the results are on the canvas.

However, what about aspiring lawyers?

There is no history of briefs you've drafted, or cases you've won. Your perceived ability to succeed is based almost solely on what law school you went to. This is, of course, nonsense, but that is a discussion for another forum.

Status management itself is a problem for firms. Work distribution can be very hierarchical. There is first-year work, mid-level work, senior work, and partner work. You'll notice that nowhere in that last sentence does actual ability for a given task play into it. Therefore, it's a problem.

Status anxiety, however, particularly when combined with a lack of trust and safety, can be disastrous.

The biggest impact is almost certainly on employee management.

Firms, and their associates, operate under a number of questionable truths. Specifically, that all associates think they want to make partner, and inevitably tell themselves that they will make partner. And that all partners think that all associates want to, or should want to, make partner. And wanting anything less is an indication of one's lack of ambition. And that not making partner is a failure of epic proportions.

**

In *How to Get Into Law School*, Estrich has a line about law students that I think perfectly sums up this notion of status anxiety.

"One day, you've never heard of them. The next day, you'd kill to work for them."[77]

Who are the "them" and "they" Estrich is referring too?

Wachtell. Cravath. Covington. Etc.

Estrich's book is in two parts: First how to get into law school; second what to do after you graduate. You can see how early the anxiety starts. As soon as you are accepted, she tells us, "you begin thinking/obsessing about what you're going to do when you get out."[78]

She continues, "There's no time to enjoy getting into law school. First, you're terrified. Then you're disappointed. Then you've been rejected all over again, for jobs you didn't even dream you wanted, at places you didn't know existed."[79]

"At places you didn't even know existed."[80] How true.

There was a funny video circulating online during my early post graduate career that meant to show an aspiring law

---

77 Estrich, Susan. 2004. *How To Get Into Law School.* New York: Riverhead Books.

78 Ibid.

79 Ibid.

80 Ibid.

student. The video is an animated robot reenactment of a typical aspiring law student talking about all the things they are going to do as an attorney. Including:

Pro bono work.

Working for a non-profit.

And of course . . . Arguing in front of the Supreme Court.

It was very funny. But this is exactly Estrich's point. "Very few people write in their law school applications that they are applying to law school because they want to be partners in one of the largest and most successful civil-law firms in America. This is not what people say in their interviews, e-mails, or conversations with faculty."[81]

I wasn't in the non-profit/public service/save the world camp, but I didn't want the firm life either. As you will shortly hear, for me, all it took was a conversation with a real estate agent about patent law to start me in that direction.

While my anxiety started before law school, most start after, when they start to hear whispers of summer jobs. For the

81 Ibid.

rest, as Estrich points out so well, "[I]t takes over like a fever from the beginning of the second semester of the first year."[82]

**

I was only slightly different.

But that was because I talked with someone prior to starting law school who gave me the scoop. When I first considered law, I thought I wanted to be an entertainment lawyer. Then when I got a job at an engineering firm, I saw myself working in-house at that firm doing government contracts.

I wouldn't say at any point that I was in the idealistic camp that so many incoming 1Ls are in. I certainly had no designs on working at a firm. But I had a conversation with a patent attorney at a mid-sized patent firm that changed all that.

I had a solid LSAT score but less-than-desirable grades, so I knew I might struggle to get into top tier schools initially.

As ranked from highest to lowest by a well known publication, the schools I targeted were: Georgetown, George Washington, George Mason, American, and Catholic. This is almost exactly how things played out.

---

82 Ibid.

I got into Catholic, American, and George Mason, but rejected by George Washington and Georgetown. So, pre-phone call, of the five schools in the DC area that I applied to, I got into the three "worst" and rejected from the two "best."

How I got this call set up, is itself, a funny story. As I said, I was thinking entertainment law or government contracts. I don't even think I thought of patent law as a thing at that point beyond knowing generally that patents existed. During an introductory meeting with my real estate agent, he asked me for my story.

"I graduated with an Engineering degree from the United States Merchant Marine Academy; sailed as an engineer on large cargo ships; and now I'm applying to law school."

This is almost literally what he said to me.

"You're an engineer and going to law school? You should be a patent attorney. I just helped a patent attorney buy a house. It was a big house. Here, let me give you his contact information."

Well alrighty then.

The call with the patent attorney felt great at the time. He seemed pretty jazzed about being a patent attorney. In fact, maybe a little too jazzed. He did evening school, which is what I was planning on doing as well. I remember hearing things like:

"The evening school professors are pretty understanding because most of them are working attorneys as well. So on nights when I have too much work, it's not a big deal to miss class."

And "I really enjoy it. Sometimes if I have an important project that I'm really into, I log back in at home after the wife and kids go to bed."

Those massive red flags aside, he did give me some great advice. Especially in view of my high LSAT / low grade situation.

"Get a job as a student associate at a patent firm so they'll pay for law school for you."

I was liking the sound of free law school.

"If you can't get that, get a job as a Patent Examiner, and then after a year go to a firm."

That works—government and private experience.

"If you don't get into George Washington or Georgetown, go to American for a year, better than Mason or Catholic because they both have harder curves, and then transfer to Georgetown or George Washington."

That sounds a little messed up. True, just messed up, but alright.

"Graduate, and get an associate offer."

I took the conversation to heart.

I've never negotiated an entertainment contract, and I've never advised a defense contractor on any legal matter.

But I was a patent examiner and practiced patent law at a firm. I finished my first year at American at the top of my class and then transferred to Georgetown. I chose Georgetown over American because it was more prestigious, and would land me a better job at a firm. And I did get an offer to work at a firm after graduation, A job I didn't even know about, not to mention want.

And I took the prestigious firm job over the government job as well. I wanted to make everyone proud. I wanted to be the big city lawyer. I didn't want to be what I perceived to be an underpaid government lawyer.

I admit that I'm glossing over whether for me, or anyone, these decisions were correct. And I think for me, long term, they were correct. They certainly worked, but there are other situations where these decisions are very clear. And status anxiety gets in our way.

**

It got in the way for Charles.

Thankfully, someone intervened.

"My friend with the contact at the Patent Office got wind that I was considering an offer from a firm. He asked to talk. He hit me with some pretty tough love.

"He said to me, 'Charles, you've worked at two different big firms. Did either work out?' The answer, of course, was "no." He continued , 'It didn't work out here, because you were not efficient enough to justify your salary. I'm assuming that was a similar issue at your first big firm?' That answer, of course, was 'yes.'

"And then he dropped the hammer, 'why do you think it will end any differently than it did with the first three firms?' And he was right. I would have just gotten fired again."

Thankfully, he took his friend's advice. And he's been happy at the Patent Office ever since.

**

Removing status anxiety will be critical to building an H4L culture, and impacts many if not all elements of the execution of H4L.

Key Takeaways

- Status management causes professionals to inefficiently and unnecessarily judge themselves and distribute work leading to status anxiety.
- Status anxiety causes professionals to make decisions about their career that may not be in the best interest of their career, health, or family.
- With better inner awareness, professionals can remove this status anxiety and can make better long-term decisions about their careers and lives.

CHAPTER 6

ENGAGING ALUMNI

"As a whole, they do fantastically, and I'm betting fairly large on them."[83]

Based on my personal experience, a quote like that is about the last thing I think I would hear from a law firm partner about ex-associates. Yet clearly not all professional services firms are created equal.

That quote above is from Paul Arnold, himself a McKinsey Alumni talking about other McKinsey Alumni. It was posted by McKinsey on the official McKinsey Alumni website.

83 Arnold, Paul. 2018. "Alumni Center". *Mckinsey & Company.* Accessed August. https://alumni.mckinsey.com/public_content/500179854.

Arnold continues, "I came to this conclusion through some pretty thorough analysis. We built a large database of founder profiles to understand who outperforms venture. We gleaned a lot of insights that define who I invest in. And guess what? McKinsey alums are crushing it.

"They are having exit rates over double the venture industry and are around four times as likely to build a startup into a billion-dollar company."[84]

**

There are two things left unsaid from above:

1. Businesses at all stages, from startups, through exit events, and beyond. All valuations from angel funded to unicorns, need consulting services. Services that McKinsey would be all too happy to supply.
2. Those businesses need ancillary services such as software support, HR support, payroll, you name it. Services that other alumni would be all too happy to supply.

While ultimately used for a chapter title later in the book, the title of the book itself could almost be called, "The Long Game," because that is ultimately what H4L is all about.

---

84 Ibid.

Because most employees leave, building lifelong relationships with employees means building lifelong relationships with the organization's alumni.

**

Conenza, a Washington state business that provides an Alumni Network software platform, recently hosted an event that included McKinsey, Microsoft, Citi, and Telstra. From that event, they identified seven critical elements of a successful alumni program (excluding networking and employment benefits):

1. Integrate your corporate alumni program into the exit process
2. Leverage executives to raise visibility for your community
3. Think global, act local
4. Offer benefits beyond jobs and networking (travel, etc.)
5. Engage with events
6. Content
7. Have an "official" network[85]

It's fair to say that this is a great list and starting point. Where I think it would be helpful to look at this a little

85 "Seven Top Tips From Corporate Alumni Leaders – Conenza". 2019. *Conenza*. https://www.conenza.com/insights/seven-top-tips-corporate-alumni-leaders/.

differently though is, instead of waiting to engage Alumni after they leave, is to engage with them while they are still employed.

**

In the most common sense, “Alumni” is a title that applies to those who have completed some kind of program affiliated with an organization.

Typically:

- School graduates
- Former employees

My undergraduate school, The United States Merchant Marine Academy (“Kings Point”), is interesting in this respect. Kings Point distinguishes Alumni from Graduates.

A slight history detour is in order. A defining characteristic of Kings Point is that all students are required to spend a year at sea, on a working cargo ship. This has been a requirement since the school’s inception during WWII, and continues to this day.

That requirement is not waived during wartime.

Accordingly, students serve on cargo ships, both commercial and military, during wartime. In all, 142 Kings Point Midshipmen were lost during WWII.

To honor those students, each was granted Alumni status despite not actually graduating from the program. This tradition continues as such that all students, upon completing their first tour at sea, are considered Kings Point Alumni, regardless of whether or not they graduate.

The practical effect of this, in the school context, is much less relevant than the potential power that this could provide in the workplace context.

**

What would it look like if firms gave associates alumni benefits *before* they left?

What would it look like if firms gave associates alumni benefits *right when they're hired*?

Let's revisit the critical elements from above. Taking out "exit process" as we're talking about advancing it even further; "having an official network" because that seems obvious; and literal benefits (cell phone plan, travel, etc.) as current employees will have them, we're left with:

1. Leverage executives to raise visibility for your community
2. Think global, act local
3. Engage with events
4. Content

Which of these would be "bad" for current associates to be exposed to? We of course have to throw in the obvious reason for an alumni network, which is networking for employment and job listings.

Where's the downside?

Remember: Employees are going to leave. Do you want them to do it behind your back or up front? Up front, you're part of the process.

Part of *their* solution, which will make them more likely to one day be part of *your* solution.

**

"Companies do not like to be abandoned any more than lovers do. Workers who quit are sometimes escorted out by security guards, their Smartphones confiscated and their email accounts deactivated. But in the professional services, former employees are increasingly treated as assets, not turncoats."[86]

"The notion was pioneered by McKinsey and Company . . . [but its] closest competitors have embraced the model. The Boston Consulting Group (BCG), for example, refers to its leavers as 'graduates.'"[87]

One look at the BCG website lets you know they do things differently. Here is a selection of some things you will see:

"Once a BCGer, always a BCGer."[88]

"To help you build . . . connections, current and past employees have access to [the] alumni network." (Emphasis added).[89]

And, of course...

"BCG alumni enjoy these and other benefits for life."[90]

FOR LIFE

86 "Gone But Not Forgotten". 2019. *The Economist*. https://www.economist.com/business/2014/03/01/gone-but-not-forgotten#ampf=undefined.

87 Ibid.

88 "BCG Alumni Network | BCG Careers". 2019. *Https://Www.Bcg.Com*. https://www.bcg.com/en-us/careers/working-at-bcg/alumni-network.aspx.

89 Ibid.

90 Ibid.

That is the essence of H4L. This is a person who you want to have a relationship with forever, because if you keep helping them, they might keep helping you. Win-Win.

From the *Economist* article, here is a crazy benefit that BCG offers its *current* employees who are interviewing elsewhere.

"[BCG] helps them to find new jobs, and even negotiate a good contract with their new bosses."[91]

Amazing!

**

So far, this chapter has been mostly about how a firm could help its alumni, and how it should offer alumni benefits to current employees. However, it's a two-way street, and that is what H4L is all about.

From the *Economist*:

"In return BCG asks alumni to help it recruit new graduates, and to brief [BCG] on the state of the industries they are now

---

91 "Gone But Not Forgotten". 2019. *The Economist*. https://www.economist.com/business/2014/03/01/gone-but-not-forgotten#ampf=undefined.

working in. And of course, it hopes they might send a bit of work in its direction."[92]

Some time ago, I was at a dinner with a number of partners and associates from different firms. At the dinner was "Joe," a partner of "Small Firm" which was an offshoot of "Big Firm 1" and then a partner "Mark" and his associate "Mike" from Big Firm 2. We were all at dinner together when a conversation about starting a small firm came up.

Joe had nothing but good things to say, "It was great! And Big Firm 1 was very supportive. They even gave us old furniture to take with us so we didn't have to buy anything right away."

There was a chorus of "wows" and "reallys?" and other things that you might expect to hear if you've ever worked for a bigger firm.

This made perfect sense to Joe though, "Yup. Think about it though. We aren't really competing against them for the massive clients. And we're too small to handle a big litigation."

All makes sense so far.

---

92 Ibid.

"So they send us smaller clients, and potential clients they have conflicts with. And we send them litigation referrals. Everyone wins."

Then Mark with Big Firm 2 comments:

"Hey there, watch what you are saying about how wonderful it is leaving the firm. I don't want Mike to get the wrong idea and think that he can start a firm."

I imagine that Mark is the kind of partner who gets livid when associates leave for other firms. Like the Partner Sam described to me.

I spoke to Mike a little later in the evening. He told me that "the irony of that situation is Mark had a relationship with a friend, I can't recall if they were classmates together or maybe junior associates together. And this friend would constantly send him work once he was in-house. Three companies in a row resulting in work going back to the partner!"

Think of all the alumni who could be doing the same thing.

**

Imagine a scenario where a former associate, or maybe even a former partner, is in-house or with the government, and is reviewing proposals for an engagement.

When they get to your response, do you want them to be thinking:

"Too expensive." Or "I would want to go through an associate I know, and I just couldn't be sure that they would get the credit (as a partner would have to be attached as well)."

Or would you rather them be thinking:

"Partner Jones is great, was really great to me during some difficult times. I have a good relationship with the proposed relationship partner. So it'll come down to rates and whether they built up sufficient associate expertise. But I can't recommend the leadership enough."

**

Key Takeaways:

- Engaging alumni is a two-way street.
- Opening up alumni benefits to current associates is critical to establishing a long-term relationship with that employee and for a smooth eventual transition into alumni.

- Alumni who are treated well as employees, but just as importantly in the run up to, during, and through their departure, are more likely to think fondly on their time at the firm, and more likely to send work, recruits, and information back.

CHAPTER 7

DEMONSTRATION

Picture this, you are at a work function, likely a retreat, with at least some colleagues that you either just met, or have known for less than a year.

The moment is about to come. You are standing there, maybe you are wearing a blindfold. Maybe you're just going to close your eyes. You're about to partake in a staple of trust building.

The trust fall.

Let's be real for a second, other than friends playing a joke on you, what are the odds that you aren't caught? Pretty close to zero. Flip it around, are you going to drop a partner? Of course not.

It logically follows that this type of event is pointless. You aren't going to trust the people any more than you did before they "put their life in your hands."

**

H4L asks employees to take a leap of faith. It asks employees to fall and asks them to trust that they will be caught, but in real terms. It asks employees to trust management with the truth.

The truth about their career aspirations.

The truth about their flaws.

In some cases, the truth about their life stories.

If an organization and that organization's management want to be entrusted with these truths, they must demonstrate that they will:

- Be honest
- Show inner awareness
- Work to remove anxiety
- Work to engage alumni

In other words, they must demonstrate trust.

**

Sticking with the trust fall analogy, demonstrating trust, is not just about honestly saying you will "catch someone if they fall." It's also about demonstrating that you can actually catch the person when he or she falls.

There is channel on the internet call FailArmy that compiles fails. I saw one that was as interesting as it was funny.

The setup is your basic trust fall, but instead of a row of people doing the catching, it was just one person doing the catching. And instead of falling backwards from the ground, the person was falling from on top of a piano bench.[93]

And instead of smaller person falling into the arms of a larger, stronger, person, it was . . . you guessed it, a person of smaller stature attempting to catch a person of larger stature.[94]

So there it was, big guy falling backwards from a piano bench into the arms of little guy. What could possibly go wrong?

Despite the obviousness of the outcome, what is so interesting about this particular fail is that there was no intention

93 "Trust Fail: Fails Of The Week (December 2018) | Failarmy". 2018. *Youtube*. https://www.youtube.com/watch?v=1UJeriMDPyk.

94 Ibid.

of it being a fail. Sure, it was poorly designed, but it wasn't a prank. The person catching just simply was not able to catch the person falling.

You can't just preach trust. Even if sincere. You have to be able to deliver.

**

The best way to demonstrate trust is to be put into a situation where at least two people are forced to work together to accomplish a common task.

Ideally, if the stakes of the situation are such that if things don't work out, then you are affected personally, and in a real fashion. How you, and those people with you in these types of situations, react will determine your trust dynamic moving forward.

Two situations come to mind that really hammer this home on a personal level.

The first story that comes to mind is professional, and deals with a fellow engineer whom I sailed with named Robert. I'll tell Robert's full story in Chapter 8, but the overview is as follows.

I was getting friendly with Robert when a combination of peer pressure, a misconception, and me being a dolt caused me to pull away, despite everything telling me that Robert was a good and trustworthy guy.

But talk is just that, talk. In fact, the motto of Kings Point is Acta Non Verbal – Deeds Not Words.

Robert demonstrated, in reasonably dramatic fashion, that I was right about him the first time. I was an idiot; he deserved to be trusted.

**

The second is domestic.

My wife and I talk about "digging deep."

This is similar to the more recently popularized term, "grit." The general concept of digging deep isn't particularly new or exciting. It's that moment when you have no energy left, but there is just a little bit more than has to be done.

You have to make a choice. Quit or dig deep.

Digging deep though with someone is one of those ways to build trust. Our first daughter had a slight milk allergy, as well as chronic acid reflux. We didn't know about either.

Now the thing to know about acid reflux in babies is that the back of their throat is burning, and more food temporarily soothes this burning. Of course, the extra food also causes the reflux to be worse. To top it off, we had to supplement with formula, which contains the milk to which she was allergic.

You see where this is going.

So, we were feeding our daughter an allergen all day, exacerbating her reflux, and then soothing her with more allergen. It was bad. She would scream for 14 hours a day. Now, before you question our parenting skills, it was our first. In addition, you have a lot of people telling you things like:

"All babies cry."

"Crying is good for their lungs."

"This is totally normal."

And all sorts of other nonsense.

In any event, a newborn is a lot of work when they do everything the way they are supposed to. So imagine adding the many hours of screaming and you can imagine how it was going. On top of all that, I was working full-time at a law firm downtown (two hour round trip commute), and was in law school.

At two, three, four in the morning, with a screaming baby is where you really find out what you are made of—whether you can dig deep. Whether your partner will dig deep, or leave you hanging.

Now, it's important to know that digging deep doesn't mean not tapping out. You never forget the look in your partner's eyes when you know they have nothing left. You know you have a little something in the tank.

"I got her. Close the door on your way out. Turn the monitor off. Get some sleep."

And they leave, and they do.

Because at some point, they'll see that look in your eyes. And shortly thereafter, you'll shut the door, turn the monitor off, and be asleep.

And you'll never be able to properly thank each other.

I trust my wife.

**

Something both of those stories have in common is the mutuality of each characters situation. Yet, that is not always the case. In fact, by definition when we are talking about a more senior-less senior relationship, there is an imbalance of power.

Trust can be demonstrated or destroyed depending on whether that power imbalance is exploited.

This brings us to the story of an associate, James, and a partner, George.

George assigned James to do three sections of a brief, and George committed himself to do the fourth section. The plan was for them to put the brief together the night before the filing.

As James recounted to me, a fellow associate popped into his office.

"What's up James?"

"Just waiting on George. We have the brief due tomorrow and I'm finished with my sections, but I need his to put it together."

"Oh, yeah?"

"Yeah, he's supposed to be dropping by shortly to discuss."

"That's pretty funny."

"Why?"

"Well, I know where he is, and I'm pretty sure you're not going to get his section tonight. Wanna know where his is?"

"Not really. But hit me with it."

"He left at 4. He had to leave early so that he could get ready for a poker tournament later tonight."

James told me he just laughed. What else would he do? Well at least one thing was the last section of the brief!

I imagine, from then on, James did not trust George at crunch time.

**

The stories above are examples of good and bad ways to demonstrate trust through actions in the actual context of work. Through shared experiences. However, the reality is you can't always demonstrate in this fashion, especially early on in a workplace relationship.

So how can we manufacture meaningful trust building shared experiences?

As we touched on in Chapter 3 with Honesty, it turns out that the key is vulnerability.

Looking back at Daniel Coyle, he spoke many times about safety and the lack of status management among the kindergartners. He also spoke about employees being vulnerable—specifically, leaders being vulnerable. From Coyle's interview for The Investor's Podcast:

"Vulnerability isn't about mushy emotions, it is about sharing information. If you are open about the mistakes you make and the weaknesses you have, you can perform better. You can share a mental model."[95]

In his interview with Adam Grant, for Grant's *WorkLife* podcast, Coyle goes further describing the relationship between vulnerability and trust:

95 Pysh, Preston, and Stig Broderson. 2018. "TIP187: The Culture Code W/ Daniel Coyle (Business Podcast)". Podcast. *We Study Billionaires – The Investor Podcast.*

"Our intuition has it backwards. You do not build trust in order to be vulnerable. When you're vulnerable, it builds trust. Being vulnerable together builds closeness."[96]

Grant goes on to describe an experiment where strangers were asked a series of personal questions like,"When was the last time you sang to yourself?"[97]

In her interview with Kara Swisher of ReCode, Kim Scott, author of *Radical Candor*, tells a similar story about an employee she calls Bob.

"We were at one of those management off-sites, where we're playing one of those stupid get-to-know-you games that everybody hates and nobody dares to admit that they hate."[98]

Trust Fall!

Bob offers up a fresh take, "This is taking a long time. I've got a great idea, we're gonna go around the table and we're

---

96 Grant, Adam. 2018. "How To Trust People You Don't Like". Podcast. *Work Life*.

97 Ibid.

98 "Full Transcript: Kim Scott And Her Book 'Radical Candor' Live Onstage For Recode Decode". 2017. *Vox*. https://www.vox.com/2017/4/13/15295070/transcript-kim-scott-book-radical-candor-live-onstage-recode-decode.

gonna tell each other what candy our parents used when potty training us."[99]

"Weird, but fast, right? Hershey Kisses right here. We all remembered."[100]

This is real. It's personal. It's not something you would just offer up in casual conversation.

It might seem silly, but it's just enough of the kind of question that makes you ask yourself, if even subconsciously, "Is this the kind of person I'm willing to tell this?"

In this case, it actually had a secondary benefit.

"And then for the next 10 months ... yeah, if ever I'm grumpy, you know what to give me. For the next 10 months, every time there was a tense moment in a meeting, Bob would whip out just the right piece of candy for the right person at the right moment. So, I liked Bob."[101]

**

99 Ibid.
100 Ibid.
101 Ibid.

Can this really work in a workplace setting? It does. These types of more personal get-to-know-you exercises are already being used.

When I spoke to Victoria Burns, Head of Human Resources at a transportation startup "TransportCo," she told me about two activities that fit this mold.

I asked Burns what do they do at the TransportCo to demonstrate that the culture is real. She told me two great stories, one example at employee onboarding, and one example that would be good for ongoing demonstration.

ONBOARDING

"When people join our company, before they start, we ask them to share two truths and a lie about yourself."

Right away, there is an important component of H4L culture embedded in this. *Before they start.* As is the case here, and as discussed with engaging alumni, it is important to advance all of this in the process.

Start demonstrating *as soon as possible* and continuously, but back to Burns.

"And then we post it to the main channel for everyone to see when we welcome them. And everyone has to guess which one's a lie. It allows you to share more about the person, and who they are.

"It's a great conversation starter.

"[For example] someone says 'I was on this movie with this actress,' and people find out that that was a truth and then they said 'wait, so you met that actress?' They'll run into them in the kitchen and have a connection around that."

This is a great way to be vulnerable. To demonstrate that you are going to lay at least a little bit on the line right from the get go. And everyone else has done it as well. So you feel safe knowing that you aren't alone.

Not only does TransportCo do this within the company's four walls during onboarding, each person also posts one truth publicly for the world to see. A quick sampling from their website:

"I participated in a competitive beatbox league for several seasons." – Potentially embarrassing!

"I attempted a start up magazine catering to the Canadian video gamers back in college. It . . . um . . . didn't work. Had a blast!" – Admitting a failed venture!

"I once managed an alpaca farm" — Intriguing!

ONGOING

Burns also told me a great story about ongoing demonstration. Ongoing activities are critical. The onboarding events are great for coworkers to learn about new hires, but not so great for new hires to learn about existing coworkers. And not so great for all coworkers to learn about those coworkers they might not interact with.

"We're hosting a BBQ where you sign up. And you get paired with two or three people. People who you have not connected a lot with in the organization.

"And each group was given a couple of questions that they were supposed to solve by the end of the event."

As an example, one question was:

"Why do you think we were grouped together?" As Burns explains it:

"People are going to go off on that! They're like 'what do you do?' 'Do you do this?' They have to learn by default."

Here is the kicker:

"[In some cases] there may be no reason they're paired together."

Here is a sampling of the questions:

1. Why do you think you were paired together?
2. Name the most beautiful place you've ever seen.
3. If you had to delete all but 5 apps from your Smartphone, which ones would you keep?

Number 3 in particular is dynamite in this day and age!

It's clear that each of the questions is designed to get people out of thier comfort zone. But also with people they don't really know.

This is great for so many reasons. Not only are they are showing some vulnerability to coworkers, and building trust. They are also learning about others in the company outside of their typical circle, which could work wonders for job crafting and other topics we'll discuss later.

**

This is truly just a taste of demonstration. As I've said, demonstration, and demonstration of trust, is really about demonstrating each of the other principles of H4L, specifically, showing employees that you are going to walk the walk.

As we move into the third and final part of this book, The Execution, I take a deep dive into the actionable elements of the H4L culture, and it will show how demonstration plays a huge role in each.

**

Key Takeaways

- H4L asks employees to open themselves up. They will only do that if they trust the organization and management.
- While shared experiences in work context are the best way to build trust, organizations can manufacture trust through various exercises.
- Those trust exercises need to be early, ongoing, and go beyond the clichéd exercises of yesterday.

PART III

THE ROADMAP

CHAPTER 8

THE H4L ORGANIZATION

Let's take a look at the roadmap.

First, we'll revisit how the landscape of business and employee has changed resulting in a need to think about employee interaction differently. And then second, we'll take a look at how some great organizations, and some great people's careers, are founded in the five principles of H4L. And third, in the next chapter, I'll give you a preview by touching on how some great organizations execute H4L, before dedicating a chapter to each of those tactical execution principles.

I – Changing Landscape. Changing Employees.

The days of lifetime employment are over. This is neither news, nor earth shattering. But it is surprising how many of the hurt feelings still persist.

I think the phrase is: "Have your cake and eat it too."

Recall the end of the conversation from Chapter 1 that Sam told me:

"It pisses me off when someone leaves to go to another firm."

"Because you're sorry to see them go?"

"No! How crappy is it that we spend all this time, effort, and money to train someone to have them go compete with us?!"

I recently interviewed a law school student in the process of deciding where she wanted to be a summer associate. This particular student had a strong interest in a specific practice of law, bankruptcy, and so was targeting firms that had well regarded bankruptcy practices.

"A number of partners have told me, 'We don't hire summer associates.'"

Now, look really closely at this next quote and compare it to the quote above.

As told to this student, on why they don't hire summers, the partners said, "We're going to invest all this money in you, and train you, and then you're just going to leave?"

Back to the student, "They're afraid that students are going to do what I'm doing, which is using a firm for experience and then leaving."

**

The reality is that, depending on your views or mindset, with sufficient time, effort, and money, you can train someone to be a great employee, and those great employees, whether those with natural talents and/or after significant investment, will always have the best options.

It doesn't seem like any organization, certainly not professional services firms, wants to get out of the "at-will" game and into the "employment contract" game. So they'll have to contend with watching their best talent walk.

You have a choice. You can yell, scream, and be generally grumpy, or you can accept it, and try to make your firm the kind of place people want to stay.

OR. OR. OR.

Make your firm the kind of place that your alumni will look back on fondly. This is the key.

Alumni should love it when they're there. Plus, love it even more after they're gone.

**

So how does H4L work again?

H4L works best with buy-in from all three core elements of the organization:

Culture – Manager – Employee

A reminder of the consequences and quirks for various combinations of buy-in with only two core elements:

- Culture + Manager – Organization may lose short term benefits due to lack of employee buy-in during that employee's tenure. But long term benefits to the organization are still possible if and when employee/ex-employee later realizes benefits.

I'm going to pause here and add something not in the earlier chapter. Look at this first combination. Only the employee hasn't bought in. What this means is the organization as a whole is doing everything to help their employees. And the managers they've put in place are implementing the culture. AND YET THE EMPLOYEES HAVEN'T BOUGHT IN.

This is almost certainly a communication problem.

At least in the next two combinations, there is some struggle against a higher power in the organization—a ruinous organization or a bad manager. If you think your firm is in this first combination, you are either wrong, or need to do some soul searching about how you present yourself to your associates.

- Manager + Employee – Organization will gain short term benefit due to employee buy-in during that employee's tenure. But may lose long-term benefits because the employee's loyalty and good will is directed to the manager, not the organization.
- Culture + Employee – This is the most challenging, and underscores the importance of manager buy-in. Organization may lose short term benefits because the employee is not growing sufficiently under poor management. But there is still potential for long-term benefits from employee if that employee has a positive impression of other managers. A common situation here would be an associate who works with multiple partners.

And what happens with all three:

Culture + Manager + Employee – Organization will gain short-term benefits from happy skillful employees, plus, the organization will gain long-term benefits from former employees who credit, not only their manager, but also the organization with their success.

**

II – A better foundation

Each of the five foundational principles of H4L: Honesty, Inner Awareness, Removing Anxiety, Engaging Alumni, and Demonstration should be practiced by, encouraged by, or participated in, by each of the three core elements of an organization.

For example, while Inner Awareness and Removing Anxiety are really the purview of employees, an organization's culture and management actions with respect to Honesty, Engaging Alumni, and Demonstration can create an environment that encourages an employee to have better inner awareness, or to have less status anxiety.

**

A. Honesty

Many if not most organizations are dysfunctional when it comes to honesty. Employees can be dishonest about their goals, plans, and desires; and management can be dishonest about employees long-term prospects, what employees need to advance, and management's own goals, plans, and desires. Creating a safe and vulnerable environment that accepts imperfection can create win-win situations for organizations, managers, and employees.

For each of the remaining four foundations of the H4L, I'll feature a story that directly hits on that element. Honesty, however, is a little different.

The reality is that most of the stories feature honesty. Many bad, but many good, and each of the good stories is really woven into the fabric of another foundational element or of the execution.

So rather than featuring a story here, I instead encourage you to see how critical honesty is to essentially every positive story retold on these pages.

**

B. Inner Awareness – Could very well be retitled "Honesty with ourselves." Young professionals, whether it's from ego, or necessity driven by the up-or-out system many firms employ, must learn to better evaluate themselves so that they can make better decisions when options are available. Also so they can better understand where they need to improve, and accept where they need to improve, which becomes critical in the execution of H4L.

Recalling what Chris Rock said in his interview with Howard Stern:

> "I kind of accepted my plight, like you did. A lot of guys don't accept their plight. They are unrealistic with where their talent is. And it's like 'Dude, you're not that good right now. That's what we have in common. I understood that I sucked."[102]

Yet, it's not just honesty with our skill level, it's also honesty with our life choices.

I spoke to an attorney, Todd Barton, who gave up, not only the big firm salary, but also the United States, and all its spacious housing, to head to Europe for a different life. I don't say easier, because as you'll see, Barton not only managed

102 Rock, Chris. 2014. The Howard Stern Show. Interview by Howard Stern. Radio. Sirius XM.

to cut his hours, but also still do the type of future partner business building that often gets overlooked when associates look to back it down.

"I usually take between six and seven weeks of vacation that I'm allotted. Still kind of on the grid, but really rejuvenating."

Barton told me that many firms' billable requirement in France are in the 1200 range; however, he still bills a fair bit above that, in the 1600 range.

The salary is much less as well.

But there's more to inner awareness than working less for less money. Home life also plays into these decisions for Barton as well.

"I live in the center of Paris." I think that sounds nice.

"I have a ten minute walk to work." Very nice.

"I don't have to worry about driving a car." I love cars, so maybe this is a negative!

"We walk to the grocery store. We walk the kids to school."

You get the picture. Inner awareness is about being honest with yourself about all aspects of your career and life.

What is your skill level?

What environment will you fit in best at the skill level?

What do you want your living arrangements to be?

It can be hard though to be honest with ourselves if we're anxious about those expectations hoisted upon us by our chosen career path.

**

C. **R**emoving Anxiety – Firms can be heavily prestige based. Relative prestige is tracked constantly and monitored, relative prestige of feeder schools is tracked constantly and monitored and some combination of those two factors for a given associate make up a significant percentage of one's impression of that associate.

A lack of inner awareness can create significant status anxiety about one's place in the industry. By removing this anxiety, young professionals can make decisions based on what's best for them, rather than what will improve their status.

It is hard for me to talk about removing anxiety without revisiting Charles, the associate I interviewed.

As you will recall, Charles had struggled at multiple firms. The leadership of my firm was not being honest with him. He was not demonstrating inner awareness, and he had severe status anxiety about what he needed to be doing.

After losing his job at the firm, Charles had an offer to be an examiner at the Patent Office. In many peoples' opinion, a perfect job for him, but it looked like he had lined up an offer at another big firm.

As we know, thankfully, his friend stepped in.

"My friend with the contact at the Patent Office got wind that I was considering an offer from a firm. He asked to talk. He hit me with some pretty tough love.

"He said to me, 'Charles, you've worked at two different big firms. Did either work out?' The answer, of course, was "no." He continued, 'It didn't work out here, because you were not efficient enough to justify your salary. I'm assuming that was a similar issue at your first big firm? That answer, of course, was 'yes.'

"And then he dropped the hammer. 'Why do you think it will end any differently than it did with the first three firms?' And he was right. I would have just gotten fired again."

He's right. At least based on the realities of most firms. If Charles had gotten past his status anxiety sooner, and accepted a lower salary/billing rate, and if the firm he was working for executed on H4L, Charles's private practice career might have been salvaged. Thankfully, because he overcame he removed his status anxiety, his patent career was saved.

**

D. Engaging Alumni – Alumni has the potential to be such a powerful tool for firms. Some embrace it, some do not. Those that embrace their Alumni network sow the seeds for a constant stream of work referrals ($$), employee referrals ($$), and enhanced reputations which can lead to both work and employee referrals ($$$$).

Employees. Will. Leave.

Just like with removing anxiety, it's hard not to reiterate a story from earlier. This time, how BCG handles alumni.

"Companies do not like to be abandoned any more than lovers do. Workers who quit are sometimes escorted out by security guards, their Smartphones confiscated and their email accounts deactivated. But in the professional services, former employees are increasingly treated as assets, not turncoats."[103]

"The notion was pioneered by McKinsey and Company . . . [but its] closest competitors have embraced the model. The Boston Consulting Group (BCG), for example, refers to its leavers as 'graduates.'"[104]

One look at the BCG website lets you know they do things differently. Here is a selection of some things you will see:

"Once a BCGer, always a BCGer."[105]

"To help you build . . . connections, current and past employees have access to [the] alumni network." (Emphasis added).[106]

And, of course...

---

103 "Gone But Not Forgotten". 2019. *The Economist*. https://www.economist.com/business/2014/03/01/gone-but-not-forgotten#ampf=undefined.

104 Ibid.

105 "BCG Alumni Network | BCG Careers". 2019. *Https://Www.Bcg.Com*. https://www.bcg.com/en-us/careers/working-at-bcg/alumni-network.aspx.

106 Ibid.

"BCG alumni enjoy these and other benefits for life."[107]

FOR LIFE

Imagine a partner at you last firm, or two firms ago, reaching out to an in-house counsel with a job lead. Even think of the benefits of a simple area get together of alumni stacked with current employees and new associates. It's such a clear demonstration for a new associate to see, in the flesh, the possibilities for their career.

**

E. **D**emonstration – H4L asks for honesty, for inner awareness, for removing anxiety and dropping the focus on status and prestige, and for engaging alumni to help new alumni, and build the firm's network. For employees to be vulnerable, and buy into the H4L foundational principles, they must trust that the organization and management will hold up their end of the bargain. Organizations can ensure this trust through demonstration.

The very literal embodiment of this is demonstrating that when an employee is honest, they don't get burned.

---

107 Ibid.

But the best way to demonstrate trust is to be put into a situation where at least two people are forced to work together to accomplish a common task.

A professional experience, one that I am at least a little ashamed about, really captures this concept.

I had recently signed on to a ship and befriended one of the other engineers, Robert. We overlapped a little bit at school together, and my gut was that he was a pretty nice guy.

But then the whispers started.

"Hey, I see you've been buddying up with Robert. You know about him, right?"

"Um, not really. Seems like an okay guy. What's the deal?"

"Well, let's just say, he might have a screw loose."

I'm ashamed to admit it, but I got sucked in.

"Really? What about?"

"I think it was a girl. Or maybe just couldn't handle the guys being guys and busting on him too much."

"Huh. Interesting."

"Yeah man, he lost it. I mean, I wouldn't worry about it. Just. You know. Keep your distance."

Because I'm being honest, I will admit that I let those stories start to color my opinion of him. This was despite my initial impression, the way he acted up until that point, and every piece of actual evidence. So I started to pull away.

Then the engine broke in the middle of the night.

Now, an engine breaking on a ship is not like your car breaking down on the side of the road. First, there is no ship AAA. We were the ship's in-house AAA. Second, there is no side of the road where we could pull off. If you're close to land with no engine, you run into that land and possibly sink. If you're in open water with no engine, you hope for good weather.

I think it was just after midnight when the alarm went off. Instinct took over and I was dressed and in the engine room in less than a minute. I turned the corner to see exhaust gas (the stuff that suffocates you in enclosed spaces) billowing into engine room (a big enclosed space).

"Shut down the main!"

"Somebody keep an eye on the generator!"

"Okay, let's see what's wrong."

We were dead in the water.

Significant portions of the exhaust gas manifold had cracked and needed to be welded, a long and extremely challenging task.

"I got it," said Robert.

I helped as best I could, but it was a one-person job, and for the most part, I, and everyone else, sat and watched Robert single handedly fix the ship. This was about six to eight hours of welding, laying down, sometimes upside down, including complicated overhead welds.

He didn't complain, all he did was stay up all night and do an amazing job. We fired the engine up, nothing leaked, and we carried on our way as if nothing happened.

I trust Robert.

**

While many of these examples of the foundational elements of H4L focus on individual behavior, these behaviors are inseparable elements of the execution of H4L. In most cases, multiple foundational elements, and their associated behaviors, factor into every aspect of the execution of H4L. The next chapter will take a quick look at each of the major elements of the execution of H4L, before taking a deep dive into each in the final section of the book.

CHAPTER 9

H4L IN ACTION

Up until this point, I have really been focused on providing an understanding of those principles that make the execution of H4L work.

So what are the more tactical Execution Principles?

Career Conversations; Performance Conversations; The Playbook; Job Crafting; and The Long Game.

Let's look at each one.

**

I. Career Conversations – Career conversations are conversations between employees and management about how an employee's career aspirations can help an organization. It's also about how the conversation can help an employee realize those goals. When employees and management have honest career conversations, then both sides can tailor the experience to maximize the benefit to all parties.

"One of the most important jobs we have is client services. They are our customers first point of contact. It's a little bit like being the information booth at Grand Central Station. It's a lot going on."

That's Ned Johnson, co-author of *The Self-Driven Child*, and he's describing the beginnings of an honest organization driven by honest career conversation.

"To handle this well, people have to be bright. And they have to be socially skilled. If you do not do either of those things well enough, it's ugly, and a lot of balls get dropped."

So he's talking about 1) a very important role that 2) requires someone with a specific set of skills. Just the kind of position where, if you find the right person, you'd want them to stay in that role for a long, long time.

Except...

"It's stressful, and kind of thrilling for the first several months. But after they settle into it, they tend to get bored. We kept having this challenge with people kind of cycling in. They are often here for a year-and-a-half and then start to get bored. And if there wasn't a position for them to grow into, they get frustrated and start grousing. They can poison the well a little bit."

This is a problem that every organization faces, and that managers face in every organization. There are some roles that require highly skilled people, which may take time and expense to train (firm associates), that are thrilling for a period (firm associates), but that can lead to boredom, repetition, and/or mental exhaustion (firm associates).

So what do you do?

Honest! Career! Conversations!

That's just what Johnson did.

"This kept happening over and over and over. So now what I've done with these folks, maybe six months in have a conversation with them."

I'm going to really break down this conversation, because it's amazing.

"'You are doing a great job at this. But my experience has been – you have to be pretty sophisticated to handle the job that you're doing – but my hunch is that in about a year from now you're going to feel like you're a little bored by this. And that's when things are going to go to pieces.'"

So far this is pretty much just a statement of fact. Just honesty. You're doing great, love you, but we've seen this happen before.

"So what I want to be doing is looking for another job for you within the organization."

This alone is almost enough. But Johnson's organization takes this one step further.

"Or, Or, if we don't see something, or if you don't think you want to be here anymore, that's fine, what we'd like to do then is say that you have a standing offer for career counseling to help you build your resume, to try to help you launch into the next stage. You're young, you probably aren't going to be here for the next twenty years.'"

There it is. Accept reality. First, this is a cool job, but it leads to burn out. Second, you're probably going to leave (at a minimum the job, maybe the organization). But the role is still necessary. The employee could still be a long-term employee. Or the employee could be a long-term ally elsewhere.

I think it's very telling the perspective from which Johnson describes why his organization does this?

"And we do this by design because it was so bruising for these people who were great until they were completely unhappy."

It's employee focused. It's not "If they do right by me, I'll do right by them." It's "I'll do right by them, and hope they do right by me."

Career conversations can be used to help employees to take ownership of their career plan. Once that plan is in place, the employee can be kept on track with performance conversations.

**

II. Performance Conversations – Unlike career conversations, performance conversations detail the *execution* of an employee's career goals. Performance conversations focus on *actionable* feedback, both positive and growth, to ensure that an employee stays on path to reach their performance and career goals, and to ensure that management is holding up their end of the bargain.

Usually this feedback comes from someone more senior to someone more junior, although it is certainly not limited to that. In fact, the exemplary story below was peer growth feedback.

I think that the vast majority of performance issues that are not 100% obvious are due to blind spots. Either a blind spot about where you may be superficially underperforming (you think you are efficient but you are not), to why you are underperforming in a known area (you know you are inefficient but can't figure out why, or how to fix).

But performance issues are not limited to traditional performance metrics. As you will see, sometimes those issues are around something more intangible.

Russ Laraway, in the *Radical Candor* podcast, tells a story about a performance conversation, albeit non-traditional, that he had while at Google.

"All of us had to take an inventory assessment . . . You [are then] put on a graph, and your behaviors are categorized around . . . three kinds of behaviors you are demonstrating to the people around you.

"There are more passive behaviors, which showed up as green on this assessment. And the passive behaviors were considered destructive.

"There were aggressive behaviors, which showed up as red on this readout. And they were also considered destructive.

"And then there were the high quality behaviors, which showed up as blue. And so what you really wanted was a nice blue circle to show up.

"I got mine back . . . and it was super green. I was seen as a more passive type person. And I didn't understand it.

"This is a very important step because now my consciousness is starting to be raised that I am being perceived differently than I perceive myself.

"Basically what I learned was from the perspective of more than one person that I was working with very closely, they actually saw me as some version of unambitious . . . that's a bad thing to be, at a number of places, and it's certainly a bad thing to be at Google."[108]

---

108 Scott, Kim, and Russ Laraway. 2017. "Ep. 23: Can I Give Feedback To Peers? Should I?". Podcast. *Radical Candor.*

First blind spot, Laraway considered himself personally to be ambitious, his co-founder of *Radical Candor*, Kim Scott, presently perceived him as ambitious, and everything in his career up to this point demonstrated that he was ambitious, and not passive.

In many cases, this is as far as it goes. The feedback may or may not be a blind spot. Maybe it's "hours are low" or "efficiency is bad," or whatever law firm issue an associate has. If left here though, two things will 100% certainly happen:

1. Unless it is super obvious, the feedback will not be addressed. Maybe the receiver will say, "What do they know, I'm ambitious! Maybe the associate will go back to his or her office and say, "I'm asking for work, I'm doing everything I can!" Whatever happens, it won't be dealt with.
2. People will form an opinion about the situation, and everyone's individual point of view on the subject will be solidified.

These two things are particularly likely to happen when the feedback is more intangible, as it is here.

In fact, I'll also talk more about a nearly identical situation that happened to a friend of mine where he was labeled as "not enjoying the law."

But for Laraway, finding this out was eye-opening, and he needed to find out why. Not so that he could argue about the results, but so that he could fix it!

"It actually had a lot to do with my decision to manifest my sense of humor just a little bit too frequently making it seem like I'm not taking things seriously.

"I was able to adjust some small behaviors very quickly once I was exposed to this perception.

"It was extremely valuable for me to have gotten that feedback . . . to address a perception gap that, if gone unchecked could have affected me in a negative way." [109]

Performance conversations are frequent touch points with an employee to make sure they are on track with both their career goals, and shorter term performance goals, by providing them with personalized actionable information about a clearly defined opportunity for growth.

III. The Playbook – Firms are unique from traditional organizations in that it is very common for associates to work with multiple senior employees. The Playbook is a way to give

109 Ibid.

new associates "cheat sheets" into various senior employees to help them hit the ground running.

Similar to the section on Honesty in the last chapter, I'm not going to go into too much detail here for The Playbook. But for different reasons. I didn't give a representative story on Honesty because honesty is really critical to every aspect of H4L – whether a foundation or execution principle – including, as you'll see, with The Playbook!

The reason, however, that I'm reserving details of The Playbook is different. The stories I tell in Chapter 12 really combine to create a new thing, and I think that is the best way to learn about and understand The Playbook.

The quick version though is The Playbook, like a playbook given to an athlete, is a toolbox of techniques to succeed at a firm. Instead of plays to outwit your enemies, they are "plays" that the organization and management freely give to new associates to help excel.

And we're not just talking about "keep your hours up," "join a local softball league," "make sure you are working with multiple partners across multiple offices (although that last one is closer).

I'm talking "Partner Smith wants his correspondence in this manner," "Partner Jones comes off in this manner but is actually easy to work with and will teach you a lot," "75% of partners did a tour of duty in an international office," "Partner Evans wants you to review your bills and make changes before submitting to her," "Partner Elliot is an ENTJ on the Myers-Briggs test," etc.

The playbook can provide employees with more real actionable information, but this time regarding the managers they work for, and about the organization they work for.

IV. Job Crafting – Job Crafting is a system where employees are given agency of some portion of their job duties. This could allow employees to focus on a particular type of work they like (reasonably common already in many firms); can allow employees to test other practice areas to explore a practice area change (reasonably uncommon); can allow entrepreneurial employees to chart their own course – for example a junior associate building business early, or an associate exploring new ways for the firm to make money (both reasonably uncommon).

From my perspective, Job Crafting is built upon the fundamental truth that everyone is different, has different likes, different strengths and weakness, and a different ability and desire to learn new things or enhance existing skills.

The fundamental problem with professional services firms is that too often the goal for every associate is to be a "superstar associate." You know the one I'm talking about: The associate who consistently bills lots of hours, efficiently, in a high margin area, with a high realization.

But A) is that right for every associate?; and B) can a firm actually operate with only those associates?

In an interview with Recode, Kim Scott, author of *Radical Candor*, recounts a story about her time at Apple. She says:

"When I was at Google I had this intense, you know, "You've gotta be on this super-fast track," and then when I got to Apple, there was an executive there who said to me, 'There's two different kinds of people who do really well on the team and the key thing to building a high-performing team is to balance the two. You've gotta balance your superstars and your rockstars.' Like, what the heck is the difference between a superstar and a rockstar?

"So I'm sort of scratching my head and she says, "Your superstars are the people who are responsible for growth and change on your team. They want new challenges, new stuff, you gotta make sure they're getting promotions fast, all that kind of stuff. Your rockstars are the people ... don't think about Ozzy Osbourne or something like that, think about the Rock of Gibraltar, they're solid as a rock. And these are the people who are great at their job, and they'll keep doing that job for years if you don't screw it up for them.

"And I realized that I had been sort of systematically undervaluing the people who were in rockstar mode for my whole career and that that was not only bad management, it was sort of out of alignment with my personal humanity."[110]

While stacking a team with superstars seems like a recipe for success, we've all witnessed how such a team is going to have gaps. This is because superstars aren't usually willing to do a variety of perceived low-level tasks.

Looking at a law firm, we can analogize this idea at both a smaller team level and also the firm level. If you are putting together a litigation team, you can't have only star orators. Unless those star orators are also fond of staying up all night drafting briefs.

And managing document review and production. And submitting filings. And . . . well, you get the picture.

110 "Full Transcript: Kim Scott And Her Book 'Radical Candor' Live Onstage For Recode Decode". 2017. *Vox*. https://www.vox.com/2017/4/13/15295070/transcript-kim-scott-book-radical-candor-live-onstage-recode-decode.

Similarly, rarely do firms specialize in only high risk, high reward cases. Most firms want to always have a variety of cases, some more sure than others, to keep the lights on while waiting for a contingency fee case to pay off.

This is very apparent in patent law, my chosen practice area. With the inevitable exceptions, firms that practice patent law typically practice both patent prosecution and counseling (getting patents), as well as patent litigation (asserting and defending patents).

Patent prosecution isn't particularly "sexy" as a legal practice. Not a lot of high stakes action, lower profit margins (relative to litigation and M&A), etc., but it keeps the lights on. I remember regularly being frustrated seeing litigation associate hours being touted despite the fact that they were often on contingency cases which could take years to pay out, or were relying on attorney fees being awarded, which is not very common.

Okay – so what do Rockstars have to do with Job Crafting? First, nothing says that superstars can't, won't, or shouldn't job craft, but here are a couple of stories that show that job crafting rockstars can be critical to the success of an organization or team.

What does Shane Battier, two-time NBA Champion, have in common with Ted Green, my childhood friend and attorney? What they have in common is that neither is a work Superstar, but they are both work Rockstars.

In an interview with Adam Grant, an organizational psychologist and host of the *WorkLife* podcast, Battier describes how he went about making himself indispensable to his team despite being less physically gifted than his superstar contemporaries.

He says, "I try to make my coaches sweat every single second that I was off the court. Saying 'how are we gonna win this game with Shane on the bench? And I need to find a way to play him more.' And you do that by doing all the things no one else wants to do. For me, that was the exciting plays like diving for loose balls, taking charges, running back on defense, being the most enthusiastic, being the most communicative, being a great teammate. Really, the things that just take awareness, and energy, I tried to be the absolute best. Cause I wasn't the most athletic. I wasn't always the best player. But those were the things that I could control to keep me on the playing floor."[111]

---

111 Grant, Adam. 2018. "The Problem With All-Stars". Podcast. *Work Life.*

I was speaking to Green recently and I asked him how he found his niche at his current firm. This is what he told me:

"For the first couple of years I put my nose to the grindstone and learned everything that I possibly could. Then you realize that there are parts of tax that not everyone knows about or not everyone wants to do. The oddball stuff, the things that take a little more thought process. There was five percent of things that others didn't want to touch. Well, if I collected everybody's five percent I wouldn't be bored and I would have something new to learn every day."

Green then went on to tell me a story about how a case came in, and it is related to an obscure area of tax law. The firm took the case. Normally when a new client or matter is brought in, there is any number of political, relationship, and expertise considerations to determine what partner might manage the client or case, or what associate might handle the day-to-day work on the case. Here's how Green described the process by which his firm handles cases related to obscure law:

"Everybody knows 'if you've not seen something before, ask Ted Green.' Everybody knows that I'm a dumping ground . . . they dump their ugly cases on me."

Battier learned to love diving for loose balls.

Green learned to love being dumped on.

A good portion of patent prosecutors would love nothing better than to close the office door and crank away. Shane Battier, Ted Green, Patent Prosecutors, and others are rockstars.

They keep the lights on so that the superstars can shine. Shane Battier is not, will never be, and should not try to be LeBron James. Battier helped James and others shine.

Job Crafting can be a tool to embrace rockstars. Or to find a place for a talented employee who is bored or struggling.

V. The Long Game – All roads lead here. Firms' existence can span decades, generations, centuries; and employees' careers can span 40+ years. Rather than being short-sighted, organizations, management, and employees should consider how each group can impact the value of each other group well beyond the initial relationship end.

The long game is really what Hired for Life is all about. As I said above, firms' existences are long. Careers are long. You can't make short-sighted decisions.

As a student associate, I went to law school part-time. While law school is typically three years, part-time takes four. However, most part-time law programs offer the option to go to school over the summer and finish in three-and-a-half years instead of four. Getting that sweet, sweet associate salary six months early is quite tempting, and I was tempted by it.

I was in a partner's office one day and this topic came up.

"Are you excited for the summer?" He said to me.

"Yes and no. Thinking about taking summer classes to try to graduate early."

Silence—followed by a look of caring derision.

"Chris, how long do you plan to be a lawyer?"

"Well, I'm thirty now, retire in my sixties, so, maybe thirty years."

"What's the rush then? What difference does six months make? You're going to be a lawyer for twenty-five, thirty, thirty-five years? Take the summer off. An associate job will be waiting regardless."

That was good advice. It was advice that I followed. And it gave me some breathing room to excel in law school, and those grades helped when the time came to find a job during the great recession.

The long game is really about how things go down during your employment that impact an employee's impression of your organization after your employment.

I interviewed two associates, who both left their jobs during the great recession. One by choice, one forced. Perhaps not surprisingly the one who lost his job thinks more fondly of the firm that laid him off than the one who quit willingly.

The first associate, who was laid off, we'll call Bob.

Here is how Bob described the time around when he found out he was losing his job.

"During my time at this particular firm, I worked primarily with three partners.

"A day or two after I learned of the decision, I walked into the first partner's office, stopped at the entrance and asked him if he minded if I closed the door. This was how he responded, 'You mean so that we can discuss this [expletive] stupid [expletive] bull [expletive] decision the other partners made about your employment? Sure, close the door.'

"I have to admit that made me feel at least a little bit better.

"The second partner organized a going away party that a sizable number of people showed up to, at a very expensive restaurant nearby, known for their expansive bourbon selection.

"But the third partner, that was probably the most special."

I asked him what about that third partner left such an impression on him. Two reasons, he said.

"First, he told the partners delivering the message to me that 'he understood that I might not want to talk yet, and I should just see him whenever I was ready.' And I took him up on that rain check. But not for long.

"Second, when I spoke to him the next day, he said to me, 'You don't really want to work here anyway.' But it wasn't pandering. It felt sincere."

Perhaps not surprisingly, Bob told me, that third party left not to long after to start his own firm.

**

The second associate, who quit, we'll call Stephanie.

Her story couldn't me more different.

"One partner came by with my door open and shouted (before I announced anything) 'Hey! Heard you're leaving! Good luck!' It was a nice sentiment."

Ok, that's a little funny. Any other goodbyes of note?

"Prior to that encounter, I met with the primary partner I worked with to give my notice. The most shocking thing about it was that it was the first time in four years I thought they actually liked me.

"He listed all the great things I did and he'd miss me doing. This was all very nice. Although I wish I'd heard more of it sooner. I don't typically consider myself to be that type of person who needs constant praise. But it's still nice to hear. And helpful."

But Stephanie then told me the real highlight of the conversation.

"He then said to me, 'You don't have to tell us, but do you mind saying where you are going?' I didn't mind, so I told him the name [Hot Startup].

"'Hot Star . . . How do you spell that.' I spelled it out. I was pretty shocked by what he said next. 'Just thought I'd run a conflict check on them real quick.'"

He ran a conflict check while she was sitting there.

That's actually the right thing to do. However, the wrong way to do it. That's thinking about the long game, but poor execution.

Bob was hired for life. Stephanie was not.

**

These were just a few examples of the execution principles of H4L The final section of the book we take a deep dive into each of these execution principles.

PART IV

THE H4L EXECUTION

CHAPTER 10

CAREER CONVERSATIONS

"The conversation about quitting ended up being the best conversation of my entire career."[112]

That's Emily Rose Schmidt from her *ThinkGrow* article entitled "Why I told my boss I was thinking about quitting."

Prior to that conversation, Schmidt had a bad termination experience.

112 Schmidt, Emily. 2017. "Why I Told My Boss I Was Thinking About Quitting.". *Thinkgrowth.Org*. https://thinkgrowth.org/why-i-told-my-boss-i-was-thinking-about-quitting-d117db4a93f4.

"The night before I was fired from my first job my boss asked me to stay late to finish up some bullshit paperwork that was definitely not time sensitive. I couldn't understand why he was pushing it, but the next day I got my clarity.

"My boss wanted me to stay late so he wouldn't have to complete the tedious task...because he had planned to fire me the next morning."[113]

On the spectrum of terminations, this is obviously the extreme end. And, similar to my own experience with honesty with management, one of the most damaging things about this experience is how Schmidt would think about management moving forward.

Suspicion and skepticism would precede every interaction.

How would she handle things at her next job? Especially when it came time to leave. On her own terms.

"I spontaneously purchased a one way ticket abroad for $150 that would take me on an adventure five months later.

"Once the ticket was purchased I had to decide what to do next. Do I leave Seer and the raise and promotion that were

113 Ibid.

heading my way? Do I jeopardize my relationships that I had built by not telling the company and then giving them a generous 4-week notice?

"I was 25, single, and healthy, without any obligations or commitments other than to myself and my company. It seemed like a small window of opportunity and I needed to make a decision."[114]

My story tracks Schmidt's in so many ways. I've been burned before by being too open with management.

"After talking to many internal confidants at Seer, I was encouraged to tell our director of HR that I was thinking of leaving."[115]

When I decided to go in-house, I too sought the advice of a number of colleagues and friends at a variety of firms. And the responses I got were mixed. Everything from, "I got my job without an iota of help from them," to "super helpful, I got placed with a client." But the reality is that most were afraid to be proactive and ask.

Could Schmidt's story end positively?

---

114 Ibid.
115 Ibid.

Of course it could! And it does!

"By being open about my potential departure and career goals I earned the respect and trust of the leaders of Seer."[116]

Now, here is the line I love most in Schmidt's article:

"Not only were they incredibly understanding of why I wanted to embark upon this adventure, they were open to finding a way to allow me to continue to work part time at Seer while I traveled the world."[117]

THAT is an employee and an organization having a solid career conversation, and that response is Seer playing the long game.

All Schmidt got is exactly what she wanted.

All Seer got is a trusting valuable employee part time (better than nothing at all) who won't feel like she owes anybody any favors, but will think positively about her company, and likely recommend that company to high quality job candidates and possible customers.

---

116 Ibid.
117 Ibid.

A critical element that Seer has here is that there is clearly organizational buy-in to having honest career conversations. This was demonstrated by confidants telling Schmidt to talk to HR. It's one thing for HR to say "come talk to us!" You might even trust them. It's a whole different thing for your friends and colleagues to come to you and say, "So and so in HR is the real deal. You NEED to tell her you are thinking about leaving."

**

Schmidt's story demonstrates one type of career conversation really well. Specifically, it wasn't clear that she was unhappy or wanted to leave, in fact it was pretty clear she was pretty happy with where she was, she just wanted to do two things that appear incompatible and Seer found a way to make them work.

But what if your career conversation involves the realization that your only option is to leave?

**

Russ Laraway, in a *Radical Candor* podcast, tells just such a story about an information technology employee, Jordan, at Amazon.

"Jordan really wanted to be a Chief Technology Officer.

"At the time she was part of a technical architect group. They sound a little bit like Amazon's Navy SeALs."[118]

I think the important thing to note here is that it sounds like Jordan is amazing at what she does, but not likely to become the CTO of Amazon.

"Her boss asked her this question of 'what is your endgame?' And Jordan ultimately confessed. 'I really want to be a Chief Technology Officer.'"[119]

How did this boss respond?

"'Great! Thank you, I really needed to know that.'"[120]

Thank you? Must need to cut some heads to hit quarterly numbers or to make some kind of Wall Street synergy target. Best of luck Jordan.

"'You work mostly on front-end stuff... But something I can do for you is I can get you working on a lot more back-end

118 Scott, Kim, and Russ Laraway. 2017. "Ep. 5: Career Conversations". Podcast. *Radical Candor.*

119 Ibid.

120 Ibid.

projects . . . Which starts to make you a more credible candidate down the line to be a CTO.'

"The boss was super clear that Amazon benefits, Jordan benefits, the boss benefits – she has a more versatile team. Everybody wins."[121]

Amazon – Jordan – Boss

Culture – Employee – Management

H4L works best when all three buy in.

**

Okay, great. We know that honest career conversations between trustworthy parties are necessary.

So you are an associate at a firm, and you have a career conversation with a partner. The likelihood is one of two outcomes: 1) I want to go for partner at this or a similar firm; or 2) My path likely involves me leaving this firm and not going to a similar firm. We'll ignore the "I don't knows."

---

121 Ibid.

The mechanics of "how to get from point A to B" for either answer is addressed more in the next three chapters (Performance Conversations, The Playbook, and Job Crafting).

But are career conversations enough?

Whereas The Long Game is in many ways the culmination of H4L, Career Conversations are the culmination of the foundational principles:

- Honesty – Obvious
- Inner Awareness – This is so critical to identifying, not only what you want to do, but what you are willing to do.
- Removing Anxiety – The outcome of a career conversation needs to be about what you are willing to do absent the influence of status anxiety.
- Engaging Alumni – Real career options from actual firm alumni.
- Demonstration – The conversation won't happen if the firm hasn't shown they're committed

To all the associates out there reading this: what are you willing to do?

The reality is that no one is going to make an associate into a partner.

That is not espousing about the impossibility of making partner. What I'm saying is that partnership is not a gift or some other type of anointing, given to you for your loyalty and years of hard work. Partnership is something that an associate has to snatch from the jaws of defeat. Because the reality is that if an associate wants to make partner at a firm, they have to take ownership of their personal partner track.

I think it's important to take a minute to dive deeper into firms and becoming a partner. So, how does one grab the partnership track by the horns? Wait, isn't it just about money? One of the predominant themes in this book is honesty so there is no sense in beating around the bush about what making partner is all about. As usual, it is in fact about the money.

At least that's what I believe. And will continue to believe until proven otherwise!

Generally speaking, the formula I presume they go with is as follows:

1. If we don't make this person partner, will they leave?
2. If the answer to Q1 was yes: If this person leaves, will we lose out on a valuable asset?

Simple. Now, that number is different for every firm. There are endless politics surrounding whether or not a particular stream of revenue is attributed to a particular associate. I believe some firms do in fact have some leeway in that number if the associate's revenue trajectory is headed in the right direction.

Especially, if they think the title of partner will help supercharge that associate's business development efforts. On top of all of that, even the most open firms closely guard the numbers here. Ignoring these facets of the partnership selection process, there are aspects that an associate can attempt to control.

A couple years ago I was joking with a friend and former colleague, now a partner, about when they would finally make a new partner.

"We'd LOVE to make a new partner. We can't find anyone willing to do what is necessary to be a partner."

If you're an associate, you're probably thinking, "Of course that is what a partner would say. Always blame the lazy associates."

If you're a partner, you're probably nodding your head in agreement.

But from another associate who also chose a path other than big law, he's right! Daniel Melo, a partner at mid-size firm, said something similar to me.

"I don't have the power to MAKE anyone a partner," Melo shared.

"I'm not a potter or a graphic designer. I don't make anything out of thin air. What we do is we RECOGNIZE that you're operating and contributing as a partner, as an owner. And we then promote you and [officially] give you the title."

I heard something similar when I was in private practice, "We know you're ready to be a partner when we think of you as a partner."

And at the time, I thought it was garbage. Nevertheless, the reality is that it's the truth.

As most firms are constructed right now, there is a set of requirements that go into being a partner. They could include: non-billable time developing business and servicing clients; handling invoices and bills; meeting the firm's standards for responsiveness; meeting the firm's standards for efficiency; billing and managing a sufficient number of hours to make you, not only profitable, but sufficiently profitable to justify giving you equity in THEIR business.

And many firms will give associates the opportunities to do many of these things. Sometimes they might be for smaller clients, but it's still a box to check off.

Listening to Melo, I became aware of two core insights he'd learned:

- How do you find out what direction an associate is heading?
- How do you prepare them for that direction?

"How we find out their direction is what any good organization should do," he offered. "We create the opportunity. And be sure the folks that are given the opportunity know it's attainable, and theirs for the deciding."

This is as critical as it is obvious.

Just like I needed to experience being an engineer before selecting that path, it's critical to experience being a partner before deciding whether that is the path you want to take.

These experiences can be being the main point of contact for a client; letting an associate take the lead on a client pitch, or a client update presentation; reviewing bills, not just of your own work but also of other associates work, ideally in combination with supervision of those associates.

"Once given the opportunity, in a controlled, safe, non-judgmental way, you get a chance for everyone to sit back and say 'hey, do I want to review work? Do I want to be the backstop? Am I interested in sitting down there and teaching another associate how to write a brief?' And it quickly becomes apparent when an associate is not interested in doing the things that I see are really necessary to take over a client, and service them to the firm's expectations. You can come to a moment of truth by providing those opportunities for people to experience what it's like to be a partner."

There is no shortage of associates that claim they want to be a partner.

Either because it's what they think they want, it's what their family thinks they want, or it's what they think they need to say to the partnership to keep their job. So the shortage isn't of associates who say they want to be a partner.

The shortage is of associates who actually are willing to **do what is necessary to be a partner**.

I had this same experience. I told myself I wanted to make partner, but neither I nor my family was willing to do what was necessary. Not because we couldn't, we just didn't really want it.

Then again, no one is going to serve you up partnership on a platter. Melo says, and I believe, that they create the opportunities, and let the associates know the opportunities are available. But, if you are an associate reading this, it is up to you to ask for those responsibilities.

Try them out. Take them for a spin. Review bills. Ask what the standards are. Service clients. Train new junior professionals. In short, **be** a partner . . . be an owner.

**

How can each group make career conversations work?

Culture – The organization can make clear, particularly through visible demonstrations, that alternative careers are not only a possibility, but are encouraged. A great way to do this is with a robust Alumni Engagement that is made available to all associates as soon as they join the firm.

Managers – Long-term senior employees not only have relationships with clients, but also a stable of associates they used to work with. Both are an opportunity to showcase where a firm career can lead. More importantly, Managers must be active in encouraging discussions with all associates (not just underperformers) about what direction their career is headed.

Employees – Take ownership of your career. H4L encourages organizations to build a culture, front-lined with managers that play the long game, offer playbooks, allow job crafting, and use performance and career conversations to maximize every employee's potential. But none of that matters if you don't participate, seek out information, and personalize a plan for yourself, which might include literally asking "this is great information on Partner Jones, but how do I use that to work better with her?" Or "I think I want to work in-house, but not for a couple years, which kind of tasks can I work on to set myself up for that while still being profitable now?"

CHAPTER 11

PERFORMANCE CONVERSATIONS

Whereas career conversations are all about the goals of an employee (whether short-, mid-, or long-term), performance conversations are all about the mechanics of improving. These conversations can and should be about both areas needed for growth to meet an employee's performance targets as well as career targets.

Performance conversations need at least three things:

1. Regularity
2. Clearly defined growth area
3. Actionable feedback to achieve growth

Before we discuss each, let's talk about a concept that is very prevalent in corporate culture, that is nearly absent in firm culture, but that could be a basis for performance conversations: the one-on-one.

One-on-ones can be a number of things, good and bad. Typically, they are an opportunity for an employee to update a manager on the status of that employee's projects – or vice versa.

But what if they could be more?

In many groups, especially smaller groups, most especially when an employee is working directly with a manager, regular updates on the status of projects can feel redundant. This would happen a lot at firm. I'm sure most have had an experience like this, or can imagine it:

9:00 AM – Joe Partner drops off marked up document at Casey Associate's office. Revisions realistically will take a day.

10:00 AM – Casey goes to Joe's office for Casey's one-on-one.

"Hi Casey, how are the revisions on that document coming along?"

"Well, you gave them to me one hour ago, and you know they will take eight hours. So I'll drop them off on your desk this evening when they are finished."

"Ok. Anything else going on?"

"Nope, you review 90% of my work, so you know exactly what I'm up to."

**

The current basis for most performance conversations now tends to be six-month or yearly reviews. Way too infrequent to effect change quickly enough. Sure, occasionally if a partner notices a low hour month, or an inefficient bill, one might get a talking to, but those are reactive and usually unproductive.

How about instead of the conversation above, we take the one-on-one and turn it into a proactive two-way performance conversation?

Now, let's look at how that could be structured.

REGULARITY

Annual reviews are the worst, for so many reasons and on so many levels.

"Thanks for making us all that money last year."

"Great year all around. Here is your massive bonus."

"Oh, and here is a list of things wrong with you."

This is not just the feelings of underperforming associates. I've known countless superstars who feel the same way. Even if the feedback is justified, it must feel wrong to get 364 days and 23 hours of praise, and then one hour a year get a list of things wrong with you that all just happens to have been written down.

Believe me though, they do nothing. They are a vehicle to get your bonus and/or find out your raise.

Therefore, we need to have honest performance conversations sooner and more frequently

Laraway, as discussed in Chapter 10, had a blind spot. Regular performance conversations are therefore necessary to identify these blind spots and fix them. TransportCo does just this. Employees have weekly check-ins that can hit both career conversations as well as performance conversations.

And not just often, but early.

This is important at a company like TransportCo which is a startup. Startups are interesting in this manner because you might have the correct skillset to do the job that is asked of you, but maybe you don't have other qualities or desires that are necessary to succeed in a startup environment. Victoria Burns, who I introduced in Chapter 7, told me about just such a situation, and how weekly one-on-ones can help mitigate this problem.

"We have people that don't have startup backgrounds . . . and there have been a few people that came in and just couldn't do it. It was too fast. It was too transparent. It was too much ownership."

This statement feels a lot like what you see at a firm. A new associate who, on paper, has everything it takes to succeed, but for whatever reason just isn't. Maybe waiting six to twelve months is too long. Could earlier and more frequent intervention make a difference?

That is what I asked Burns. "Do you make any early attempts to rehabilitate?"

"Definitely. Always try to rehabilitate first. Did they miss something in the interview? What are you thinking? Understand their expectations?"

Note what is also really interesting here is that the thought process is employee focused. What are YOUR expectations?

"A leader, with each person on their team, does a weekly touch base with everybody."

The next is the line I like the best from my interview with Burns:

"You should never be more than a week away from the last conversation."

Conversation = Performance/Career Conversation.

I'm sure they are regularly talking with their leader. This is a formal "how are things" and that is great.

"If there is an issue week 1, and they are not getting it. They're ramping, it's ok. Week 2 – You know what, they aren't seeing this, we talked about this in the last meeting. Week 3 . . . A month in, they aren't getting it. Let's get them some better feedback."

Later, in Chapter 13, I share a conversation with Burns about how these conversations can be amazing opportunities for Job Crafting.

CLEARLY DEFINED GROWTH AREA

Regular conversations need a very specific element to be worthwhile: They must provide actionable feedback.

Laraway had a blind spot, identified that blind spot, and then was able to change his behavior to address that problematic behavior, but what if a blind spot is identified and you either aren't given actionable feedback or the person delivering can't articulate feedback?

Think about what we just discussed with respect to how to make partner at a firm. If you ask a partner what you need to do to make partner, the two most common things you would hear would be, "You'll make partner when we think of you as a partner," and "Just focus on being a better lawyer, and the other stuff will come." Now, both of these are one-hundred percent true.

But they're also potentially worthless comments if not accompanied by:

1. A list of things that you can do that will make other partners think of you as a partner. And what the expectations are for each of those things. And
2. A list of things that you can do to be a better lawyer. And what the expectations are for each of those things.

If you are a partner at a firm, you might look at these two things and say: "there isn't a list," or "it's more of a feeling," or who knows what other comment.

Nonsense. We just made a list in Chapter 10: review bills, review junior associates work, and take ownership of client relationships.

Act like a partner, be a better lawyer, and my two other common refrains, bill more hours and be more efficient, are potentially problematic because they can sit at two different levels of unhelpful. First, they are very high-level comments (think: "you need to lose weight"). So they lack any specificity. Then even when more specificity is given, the reasoning behind the steps isn't given, or the steps still lack sufficient information to make them actionable (think: "eat less carbs" or "you should do pro bono, but not too much pro bono").

A lawyer and friend was recently telling me about this kind of feedback that impacted him. James was the subject of some internal mid-cycle reviews and his direct supervisor wanted to give him feedback from those reviews. That conversation went something like this:

"James, some people have the impression that you don't actually like litigation."

"What does that mean?"

"No clue."

"Should I stand in the lunch room and loudly discuss a recent relevant Appeals Court case on standing to sue?"

He wracked his brain but couldn't think who could possibly have said this about him. However, even beyond that question, what did it mean?

So very unhelpful.

James continued doing his job for the next couple of years, doing it well, and to positive subjective reviews and objective rewards via compensation. After this time, and some management changes, James got another review. As he told me, it went pretty similar to the last one.

"Everyone thinks you do great work, but the chief litigation counsel feels that you don't really enjoy the practice of law."

I'm picturing James's jaw hitting the floor.

As James told me:

"It's clear that the Chief Litigation Counsel was the person who gave the initial "don't like litigation" feedback. Which was pretty shocking because I haven't worked with him often, but the feedback was always very positive. Also, many of those encounters were critical issues, with short time frames, and often interrupting nights, weekends, and vacations, and all of which ended in success."

James and his boss, have a plan, but impossible to know without knowing exactly what is meant by "not enjoying the practice of law."

**

Annual feedback is problematic. Anonymous feedback can be as well. In order to be anonymous it has to be reasonably general, which is, as discussed, extremely unhelpful.

Annual feedback isn't particularly helpful because the person receiving the feedback could theoretically have been doing something wrong for eleven months and not even know it. Worse still is that person can be doing things correctly, but there is a misunderstanding and so the reviewer thinks the wrong way to a person's detriment.

I spoke to an associate, Joe, about just such a situation.

"I walked into my annual meeting anxious. It had been a good year, but I still braced for the constructive portion of the review. That portion was pretty much 'someone indicated that you *seem* unwilling to take on work.'

"This surprised me, I genuinely don't remember passing up any work. I'm always willing to take on work to maintain my hours. So I asked for clarification.

"The clarification made it extraordinarily clear that one particular attorney, Ryan, must have made this comment. I'll admit I was probably more direct than I should have been. I pretty much said, 'So, Ryan then?'

"The reviewers stumbled out a 'No, no, not necessarily. Could have been a couple different people.' But it was clear. I told them that 'I've asked Ryan on multiple occasions if he wants me to do any work for him.' Their response to me was pretty shocking, 'Maybe it wasn't so much that you ever declined to do work, but rather that it might have just been a 'feeling' that you didn't want to take on any work.'"

There are two issues with this. First, depending on when Ryan first thought this, it could have been up to year for Joe to find this out. Second, Ryan has formed an impression of Joe, that may be wrong, for that period. Worse Ryan shared it with the partners.

This situation failed both the regularity component, as well as the specificity component.

I don't think Ryan did anything wrong here, and I don't think Joe did either, he was working in a system. I think the system can be improved.

Here's the thing, Joe one hundred percent could have given Ryan this impression. Maybe Ryan gave Joe a project and he expected it to be done in four weeks and it didn't get done until six, and he interpreted that as Joe prioritizing another attorney's work.

If Joe was having regular check-ins with Ryan, they could have talked about. Joe could have explained the timeline. He could have done things better. And he told me as much,

"I should have been more clear to Ryan that I liked his work. I should have said 'thanks for putting me on this project Ryan, super interesting topic. Please let me know if you have any more projects like it.' That could have been enough to avoid all of this."

But even if this conversation had happened sooner, and the area of growth was clearly defined, it still also lacked actionable feedback.

ACTIONABLE FEEDBACK

In any workplace, feedback is critical to improvement; however, not just any feedback. Feedback must be useful and actionable. In order to get useful and actionable feedback, the actual problem has to be known. Just about every big firm attorney has heard the following phrases: "Just bill more hours," and "Just be more efficient." What in the heck does that mean?

Yes, it seems obvious that if you are 20 hours short per month, and 20 hours of extra work is available, that an associate simply needs to do that extra 20 hours worth of work. Similarly, although not as easy, if you are overbilling for a task, or even billing an appropriate amount for a task if you are expecting to get promoted a class year, then you need to cut out wasted time or otherwise improve your efficiency (for example, get better at your work).

However, the reality is that there are any number of reasons that an associate might have low hours: not recording hours properly, cutting their own time, personal problems keeping them from work, lack of mastery leading to work paralysis, and yes, being lazy. Similarly, there are any number of reasons that someone might be inefficient: trying to juggle too many projects, poor task management, misunderstanding of the task, misunderstanding of quality expectation of the work, again – insufficient mastery, and yes, lazy or otherwise, a bad worker.

As you can imagine, this can overlap significantly with Clearly Defined Growth Area. Sometimes just defining what is actually wrong solves the problem!

For an associate low on hours, for any reason, hearing "bill more hours" is worthless. The only thing it could possibly do is make the associate aware that they are on a partner's RADAR as being low on hours. Otherwise, no help. Another scenario would be to give an associate feedback on improving hours for one problem when the associate has a different problem. Neither of these is helpful because neither addresses the actual problem.

**

After many successful years at a large international general practice firm, Paul Jacobs co-founded a firm with the express intent of doing things differently. It was an opportunity to build a firm from the ground up using many of the H4L principles (whether or not he even knew it!).

One area that I think bigger firms have an opportunity to improve is handling underperforming associates. I'm not talking about some all-time bad associate; more an associate who is struggling in an area.

Before I talked to Jacobs, I assumed this was the type of situation that having your own firm would allow one to improve on. So I was really excited to talk to him about how he and his partners handle this situation.

We talked a lot about feedback.

"We found out that the best way to do this is to just ask the associate 'what is holding you back from making your hours? How can we help you make your hours? What's going on? What are the problems you are seeing? What is going on that is preventing you from billing this task at the appropriate amount of hours?'."

The most important thing about these questions is that it is starting a conversation with the associate. It's not stating a truth that everyone knows (someone has bad hours), but rather it's attempting to figure out why. That alone is a potential game changer.

Jacobs told me about a venture fund associate with whom he was working.

"There's an associate right now that I'm working with, and I've never had to do this before. Every single month this associate would come in way under hours. This person had built a giant hole."

I suspect most start thinking here lazy or lack of work, maybe neither.

"After trying all different ways to get it going, I finally had a long talk with this associate. I asked 'what do you think is holding you back?' We talked a lot about recording hours, writing time down, which is something this associate has never had to do before."

Unfortunately "Things associates never had to do before" didn't quite have the same ring as Hired for Life, otherwise I might have used that for the title. This is such an important concept in the professional services industry and really in the work force in general.

Whether you are a first time associate, or a first time corporate employee, there are myriad things that you literally have never been asked to do before. They sometimes seem second nature after ten, twenty, thirty successful years at a firm, but they are not obvious.

Here, then, was Jacob's solution.

"'Ok. Here is what we are going to do. At the end of the day, after you've recorded all of your time, I want you to send yourself an email with your billable number for the day in the subject line, and then on Monday morning I want you to send me an email with your total for the prior week.'"

Brilliant.

"The daily email is just so that it is on his mind. What do I do with the weekly email? Maybe I glance at it, 7 hours, cool, delete it. Maybe I don't do anything with it. It's just a way of training this associate. It's worked wonderfully . . . and this associate is appreciative. Nothing was working. This associate was just not attuned to, throughout the day, putting time in.

"Was the associate working the hours? Absolutely. Just didn't know how to keep track of it."

That next month was the associate's best.

**

Other issues can involve a combination of factors, like budget, client exceptions, and associate misunderstanding, to not only create a problem, but also make it difficult to determine the root cause.

Legal bills can get high fast, and not every client wants the same level of service. In one situation, the client might want the whole firm working day and night on the case, in another they might not want a first year to put in more than an hour.

Jacobs told me about another associate who was doing great work but maybe missed on client expectations.

"An associate was billing wildly on a legal opinion for a fixed fee client."

In other words, a client has said, "I'm going to pay you X, and I know that means you will only spend Y hours on it. That's fine."

"This associate would sometimes bill a couple of days on these opinions, when really they should only be taking a day or so."

Again, "spend less time on these," wasn't working. So what did Jacobs do?

"Show me what you do. And we walked through what this associate did. And I said 'Okay. So here's what you do.'

"It would have never worked if I walked in and said 'Hey, you can't bill 30 hours on these opinions. You can only bill 10 hours.' That's not going to teach this associate anything.

"People who are in their first or second year, how do they know?"

**

How then can each group make performance conversations work?

Organization – Make it part of the culture to encourage regular feedback throughout the year. Establish weekly one-on-ones. In situations like a law firm where associates work with many partners, the associate can rotate through the partners every couple of weeks.

Managers – First — and this is the single most important thing in this chapter — be present. Do not cancel the one-on-one. Second, ensure that during the one-on-ones the employees know that it is their time to talk about whatever. Third, proactively make sure that the associate knows where they stand with their career and performance goals and give actionable feedback regarding clearly defined growth areas.

Employees – You must be proactive. As we discussed in Chapter 10 – no one is just going to make you partner for time served or General Counsel or whatever title you aspire to. Ask, “I want to make partner here, is there something I can do this week to demonstrate partner-like traits?” Ask, “I’m having trouble getting my hours down on this particular type of project, can you help me work that out?”

CHAPTER 12

THE PLAYBOOK

"With this particular partner, I noticed from his build that he must work out a lot. He had a younger vibe to him, he'd go get drinks. Given his vibe, and knowing he was into exercise. I would plan a happy hour and invite him.

"Our offices were just two doors down from one another and I'd drop by and ask him questions. As our relationship built, I would say 'hey, you go to this other gym, why don't you try CrossFit?' I brought him there and he liked it. And then he invited me to the gym that he was going to."

That's from Cory James, co-founder of a boutique healthcare law practice in the southeast, from a conversation about how he sought to build a relationship with a partner to help him succeed at a big firm before opening his own firm.

Wouldn't it be great to have a cheat sheet that tells you the ins and outs of a firm and its partners before you need it? Without having to literally size up a partner at meetings.

I think that associates could use a playbook.

In football, each player is given a playbook that includes every play they might need to know that can be used in a game plan versus another team. Now, the playbook I am talking about is a little different, as will be explained.

In addition, it is also going to be used to work better with one's colleagues rather than to defeat an enemy.

**

So what is a Playbook?

A playbook is a combination of general actionable tips and techniques for working at a particular organization combined with information on various partners and managers to assist associates in working with those partners and managers.

One element of the playbook came to me from Lydia Murphy, a partner at a large national law firm. Murphy was telling me about aspects of her firm's new associate program, a program that goes on throughout every associate's first year at the firm.

“We have a compendium that we compiled. We used to make them read books . . . [but we realized that] none of these books were really ‘us’.”

The first suggestion to Murphy was “we should write our own book?” I like her solution better.

“Then it hit me: why don’t we get letters?”

“We compiled these letters, and every year I ask more partners to write ‘Dear Associate’ letters. They talk about things they wish they had known their first year, and things that they have experienced.”

They could be anonymous or signed. They can be on substantially any topic.

“When you read them . . . you can see the culture come through. It’s really cool. It might be ‘here are my five points for success,’ or ‘here is where I messed up,’ things like that. . . There is a really strong firm culture that shines through.”

It was a smashing success.

**

At a certain size, bigger firms start feeling less like a single organization and more like a collection of smaller firms, each of those smaller firms consisting of a single partner. This is true even when working with multiple partners on a single-deal team or single-litigation team. When you are new to a law firm you are learning, at least:

1. The general ins and outs of being a law firm associate, like billing time and efficiency;
2. How to build up a sufficient workload to hit your hours;
3. The actual practice of law (i.e., not law school law);
4. How each and every individual partner, of counsel, and higher-level associates want you to practice law and manage time; and
5. How to manage working for multiple senior attorneys.

Moreover, it can get much more nitty gritty from there. How to properly work to a budget or flat fee? How to handle bills.

When I first heard about Murphy's letter system, I was blown away. It seems so obvious, but it is something that I've never seen done. Sure, there are any number of ways to get general advice about how to conduct yourself at a firm, but nothing this specific. Nothing comes from the actual partners that you will be working with.

The letters can also be the basis for general training. If it looks like a number of partners give common advice maybe that is something to have a whole program on during orientation.

I also want to stress again here that the advice in these letters should be actionable! Think of these letters the exact same way that you would think of a performance conversation or a career conversation. They must give actionable information on a clearly defined topic.

**

If you think of attaining partnership as a competition, what better way to win than to get the other team's playbook?

Now, in a regular competition, you wouldn't want to give out your playbook. However, making partner is not a regular competition. A common refrain you hear partners make is that they want every associate to make partner. So if you want someone to "win," why not just give them a cheat sheet?

**

But a playbook is more than just advice.

The second part of the playbook is learning about the partners themselves. For this, we can look to the consulting world.

Bain Consulting regularly makes lists as one of the top places to work. Sure, the salaries are high, but it's still an intense environment, and the consultants seems to genuinely enjoy working there.

What makes Bain different? One way is with a new program that is starting to make its way through the company.

For his Work Life podcast, Adam Grant spoke with Or Skolnik, a principal at Bain to learn about how Or brings a new team up to speed on something of critical importance: How to work with Or.[122]

Or tells Grant "[I give everyone] a one-page overview of working with me, and it's written by people who have formerly worked with me."[123]

As Grant describes it, Or "Asks his colleagues to describe his personality and the most effective ways to work with him." It's like an 'operating manual, kind of like the one in your car – only for a human.'"[124]

---

122 Grant, Adam. 2018. "Your Hidden Personality". Podcast. *Work Life*.
123 Ibid.
124 Ibid.

Just like the letters above, something so obvious. When I hear these things my first thought is "people have to be doing this, right?" I don't think so.

Even Grant was "kind of stunned that every manager on earth doesn't do it." Specifically saying, "These are things you would learn in six months anyway. Why would I not want to know them on day one?"[125]

Not only that, why wouldn't a manager want you to know that on day one? Wanting a new employee to struggle and flounder to figure out your opinion on the Harvard comma isn't some fun and amazing test of that employees "grit" or whatever other trait you might be testing.

It's a waste of everyone's precious time. Time that could be spent billing.

I remember one of the very first things I ever turned in to a partner for review. I assume it was my first week at the firm, maybe early in the second. It was a simple enough task. As a reminder, I was an engineer by trade but not even a desk engineer; I was an elbow-deep-in-oil kind of engineer.

125 Ibid.

And while I better appreciate the importance now, at the time I just didn't focus as much on my writing. I finished a draft of the task, reviewed it quickly but didn't want to waste time (already worried about that efficiency!), and I turned it in.

I got a call within a couple of hours calling me to the partner's office. We'll call the partner in question Arthur. At the time, Arthur and I were on opposite ends of the spectrum when it came to the use of English. I remember hearing something along the lines of:

"Chris...um. So what are... ok...what are you saying...

"I got to be honest with you. The content of this looks fine, but I simply can't review this as it's written. Take the time to fix the little mistakes and bring it back."

What if I had some information on Arthur? "Make sure anything you bring to Arthur is mistake free. Like seriously 100% mistake free." Maybe I would have taken an extra ten or twenty minutes. Or better yet, had a colleague give it a five-minute once-over.

The other difference between this and the letters is that these operating manuals are not necessarily written by the partners about themselves. It could certainly be helpful for them to include their own thoughts on how to work with them. But

I think it is critical for this to be third party information—colleagues and associates.

**

A final optional element of the Playbook could be any one of the various psychological evaluations of management. McKinsey for example uses the Myers-Briggs testing for all of their employees.

Murphy's firm has their partners do the DISC analysis. DISC is an acronym for Dominance, Influence, Steadiness, Compliance. Combinations of these traits could further identify a person as Task Oriented, People Oriented, Outgoing, or Reserved.

Where a person falls into the various categories can help you with how you approach someone.

**

So then what is The Playbook?

The Playbook should include some combination of:

1. Actionable advice on specific topics from management to employees about how to succeed in the organization,

in specific roles within the organization, and/or with people; and

2. Operating manuals specific to managers; which may or may not include:
3. Personality analysis for those managers.

How awesome would it be to have a playbook for each partner?

This is all information that you need to know anyway, and if you want to succeed will need to find out eventually.

As Grant says: "Why would I not want that on day one?"[126]

**

How can each group make The Playbook work?

Culture – Demand might be a strong word, but an organization should encourage all managers participate in the process. Provide a letter or equivalent, have a 360-degree review system or equivalent in place, and, if applicable, offer personality testing.

Manager – Don't be afraid to put yourself out there. Everyone has an opportunity to review, and any sort of 360-degree

126 Ibid.

feedback is an opportunity to learn about a potential blind spot to increase your own performance, and make sure that any advice you give in a letter is actionable.

Employee – **Use the playbook!** It's pointless to have a cheat sheet and not use it. Employees also have an opportunity to help keep the playbook up-to-date. If you notice something wrong, think something has changed, or want to offer a conflicting comment, do so.

CHAPTER 13

JOB CRAFTING

I'll never forget when I walked into my Intro to Engineering class. This class was one of two classes we took to determine whether we wanted to go the transportation (logistics/navigation) route, or the engineering route.

I went into school dead set on engineering, but I started having second thoughts after learning more and more about the transportation route.

We all walked in, and sat down. Professor Franklin walked in looking a little bit like Doc Brown from *Back to the Future*.

Instead of stopping in the front of the class he just kept going. "Follow me!"

He took us out to an alley behind the engineering building and circled us around a little cylindrical device mounted on pallet. The device had a pull start cord.

He pulled it.

The device was not just any device; it was a small kerosene fueled turbine engine. The pull starter cord made it like a little lawn mower engine from hell.

And wow did that baby scream!

I stood there, mesmerized. Any thoughts about picking transportation were blown out of my brain by the sound of that engine wailing in the alley.

**

How do you find out what you want to be when you grow up?

I have many early memories of tinkering with things—building Legos (usually following by destroying them on video in slow motion), forging axes and knives with my grandpa (Yes, my grandpa had a forge in his backyard), restoring cars with my uncle in the basement of his business. It was no surprise that I decided to go to college to be an engineer; but the reality was, I had no idea what the profession of engineering would be like.

This presents a problem.

Kings Point, is a federal service academy, like the Naval Academy, that pretty much only has two majors: Transportation and Engineering. Moreover, once you decide, you are pretty much stuck. Professional Schools are very similar in that once you decide to go; you pretty much are agreeing to be a lawyer, or an accountant, especially if you ever plan to pay off the debt.

Kings Point, however, offers two key differences. First, all students take a transportation course, and an engineering course, before they choose which path they take. Second, all students complete a first cadet period at sea before they are locked into their federal commitment. Regarding the first, you might be thinking: can one single class really give you a good idea what it will be like?

I'm the perfect case study. As I mentioned, I went in fully planning on being an engineer. But once you're there, you start having second thoughts. If you were a transportation person, you start hearing about how engineering offers better long-term job prospects. If you were an engineering person, you start hearing about how transportation is a whole lot easier, you don't have to be in a dark, dirty, and hot engine room, and that transportation is more of a "business" degree.

I fell into this trap. When a 17/18 year-old hears about being a business person, dollar signs start flashing. The prospect of sailing around the world (cool!) covered in oil and grease (not so cool) starts to set in. I think it was good then that I took my transportation intro class first. And by the end of it, I admit, I was close to being sold, but you know how that story ended.

The feeling I had listening to that engine scream is probably the same feeling that an aspiring undergrad or law student feels like when watching a partner in court. However, just as listening to a blistering jet engine has little to do with the actual job of being an engineer, watching an inspiring court performance has little to do with the actual job of being a law firm attorney.

Thankfully, Kings Point has a second component to the training that helps you get a really good idea what the job will be like. All students spend a full year on a real ship as a cadet, being an engineer. This experience is nearly opposite of what a summer associate experiences at firms.

First of all, pay as a cadet is awful. I think when I was a cadet in 2000, cadet pay was something on the order of $450 per month, just a tiny bit less than the first year associate pay that most summer associates get. Second, my time as a cadet included work that was nearly identical to the type of work I was doing later when I was an engineering officer. If something went wrong in the middle of the night, I was called to help. If a maneuvering operation into port happened to be taking place at 2 a.m., I was down in the control room.

In other words, I had a pretty good idea of what I was getting myself into.

Compare this to some of the things that I've been told through the years about how to treat summer associates— "Don't give them any work with tight deadlines," "Don't give them any long projects that they might not be able to finish," "Don't give them any busy work like document review," "Be sure to bring them to client meetings and depositions."

Which could be interpreted as— "Don't let them know what it's really like to be an associate at this firm."

Some of this is practical, and I don't fully fault the firms for these choices. Summers are under intense pressure to attend endless events that I know start to get really old, really fast, so a tight deadline could be unrealistic; work that goes unfinished is work that someone else will have to finish, sometimes from scratch; and by actually going on client visits and to court, and by not doing doc review, a highly sought after associate might be more likely to pick your firm.

That doesn't change the fact that the first day at a law firm for associates is the first time that they are doing and seeing the kind of work that will make up a good portion of their career.

None of this is to say that my first day as an engineering officer was any less frightening. That first night where I was solely responsible for a watch was terrifying.

I had no idea what to do. However, I generally knew what it was about. It just then became about learning the specifics of the ship. It wasn't about learning what the job itself was, and if I hadn't enjoyed my experience at sea, I could have pivoted. If I realized soon enough, I could have switched schools. Or if I still liked the program but didn't like the job, I could have looked into "shore side" engineering jobs, or active duty military.

I had options.

The first time most law students know what they've really gotten themselves into is after the final check for law school has already been written.

**

What then is there to do?

Job Crafting.

Job crafting is a phrase that's being said more and more frequently in employment circles. Typically, when used, it refers to giving employees significant freedom to shape the type of work they do on a day-to-day basis and/or direct their career within the company.

For purposes of H4L though, job crafting includes a second critical element: assisting employees with finding a better fit outside the company if appropriate.

SHAPING WORK/CAREER WITHIN ONE'S ORGANIZATION

Victoria Burns, HR executive at TransportCo, described to me an example of job crafting that they use.

"The largest part of our team is software developers, and one of the things that our Chief Technology Officer has done really well is that she created three different tracks."

The work "track" jumps out at me right away based on the common usage of "Partner Track" in the firm world.

"She created a track that is a managerial track, she created a track that was an individual contributor, and she created a track that is an integrator that works across all of the different departments. She created three different roles that people could say 'you know what, I'm an individual contributor,' or 'I want to lead people' – so you go that track."

You'll remember from our discussion of superstars versus rockstars, that the typical career path is some combination of "Everyone needs to be a superstar" and "Everybody needs to be pushing towards management." In this typical type of regime, you end up with two classes of employees with little choice: management track, and individual contributors who went off track.

The parallel in the law firm world is no different: Partner-track and waiting to quit or get fired. While more and more firms are starting to offer viable long-term non-partner-track attorney positions, historically very few firms offer such a genuine non-partner track. And when they do, the perception can be that you are a second-class citizen.

I asked, "Are the tracks fluid?"

"Yes!"

Job crafting is not always initiated by the employee. Hopefully, when it's employer, or even friend, initiated, it's a conversation about optional ways to make your job a better fit rather than forced changes. Burns told me about one employee who was actively trying to craft.

"She just seemed like she wasn't happy doing the work anymore, and she had been doing the work for a while. She had been doing the same role. She's taken on some different things within her role.

"To her credit, she's even created a bunch of projects that she wanted to work on. She wanted more exposure to different executives. She wanted to be more involved in different areas of the business. So she created projects around it.

"We know she wants more," Burns said, "So the conversation is turning to 'what's the more? I'm not sure that we have the more. But let's hear what you're looking for so that we can craft it for you.

"Now, we're working through that."

But it's rarely going to be all roses. And as an employee, that is something you have to accept.

"Maybe part of moving forward is that you have to do some things you don't like. . . . But as long as the bulk of it is the stuff that you enjoy . . ."

**

Ok, so how could we apply this to a firm setting?

It would be disingenuous to say that these types of conversations don't already happen at firms. Associates can have billable hour requirements adjusted, class years adjusted, and can work on different types of projects. And generally speaking, within the bounds of meeting one's hours and efficiency targets, associates have a lot of freedom to work with the partners they choose.

Many times these changes are forced. However, they could just as easily be options that associates could choose to take to better fit long term in a firm.

It is critical though for there not to be a stigma associated with going down an alternate route, especially if the goal is to make the tracks fluid. I know from speaking to any number of associates that they felt taking a reduced hours requirement, or skipping a class year bump would kick them off the partner track.

Those feelings are real, and I think the feeling often reflects reality. Why?

If a firm believes an attorney needs 16,000 billable hours and a $500,000 book of business to be considered for partner, why does that matter if they get there in 8 years or 12? Or 15?

And that's just with variations to a typical partner track.

A firm could easily apply TransportCo's software developer model to the associate model as follows:

Manager = Partner track (Build business, manage clients, associates, and larger cases, and crank away when necessary)

Integrator = Of Counsel track (Manage clients, associates and cases of any size, and crank away when necessary)

Individual Contributor = Associate track (Crank away, manage smaller cases and clients as desired)

The first couple of years of any of these are likely pretty similar. As it comes time to make some decisions, a firm following the H4L principles can lean on Career and Performance Conversations to help steer associates to the right track.

**

CREATE OPPORTUNITIES OUTSIDE OF ONE'S ORGANIZATION

There are two ways to view creating opportunities outside of one's organization.

A. Arming an employee with the skills needed to take their career to the next level internally or externally.

This might take the form of giving an employee more of a certain kind of work that they might encounter in a different environment. For example, in the firm environment, I rarely saw indemnification clauses, and only saw ownership/title clauses when a merger or similar deal was taking place. Those two types of clauses are probably 90% of what in-house intellectual property counsel review when asked for contract support.

What if it's not possible to give that kind of work to an associate with in-house aspirations? Maybe invite an in-house counsel to come in for a hands-on seminar, direct the associate to high-quality continuing education on the topic, or look for an opportunity for the associate to do a secondment with a client.

B. Recognizing when the employee may need to move on.

Don't interpret this heading as forcing someone out. It might simply be "this is the closest we can get to what you want, and we are happy for you to do that. But if you still want more, then we'll help you find a better fit."

I cut off two of Burns' quotes that I will finish now:

"We know she wants more," and they would like her to keep working for them "if we have that more."

The reality is that a particular organization might not be able to offer the "more" that an employee needs, and I think that message is important to be delivered. I think it's safe to say that Burns agrees.

She said, "We might have to say to someone 'we don't have that track here. But why don't you stay here and do this role as long as you like?' The problem is that most companies won't say that. And you also sometimes get a negative reaction from the employee when you say that." However, if you want to leave, we'll will help you "make connections elsewhere so you can do it."

To all the employees and associates reading this, this is where inner awareness and reducing anxiety come into play. If there is a characteristic or trait that you want management to demonstrate, you must also demonstrate.

You can't say you want to be a partner. Find out what needs to be done. Ask for the support necessary to do what needs to be done, **not** do what needs to be done, and then be surprised when it doesn't work out.

When I was talking to Burns, she said something to me that I, of course, thought of a lot.

"Could you have done something different? Yeah, but did you want to? You probably didn't want to."

And she's right. As I've discussed before, I probably didn't really want to be a law firm partner, and that is a valid choice. In fact, within reason, any choice is a valid choice for any particular person's career.

But you have to make that choice.

Burns told me about those conversations as well. When job crafting with an employee, she might say, "Is this even what you want in your life." She tells me that sometimes the conversation with an employee is not about how to craft this job to fit you better, but rather whether this is even where you should be. She goes on, "The conversation might be 'you say you want to live here, you want to spend time with your family, you want more time outdoors. Is this really what you want?'"

How do you find out what you want? Performance Conversations, Career Conversations, Job Crafting. But that is still at a particular point in time.

Which leads us directly to Burns' closing comment to me: "Sometimes people can't truly know what they want. I don't ignore that piece, I just assume 'well, that's what they want right now.' Part of it is the evolution of what you think you want in your life. It's a wonder that we companies get it even right part of the time."

**

How then can each group make Job Crafting work?

Culture – The organization is in a position to make it a directive to allow the kind of flexibility necessary for job crafting. This might include relocations to be closer to a particular partner or type of work. The organization can also craft training programs to set the tone that broad and diverse skill sets are encouraged. And also treat new employees like future alumni. Open up Alumni resources to all employees immediately.

Managers – Demonstrate. Demonstrate. Demonstrate. When an employee has the courage to say, "I'd like to do some things a little differently. Go out and set them up with a different partner. Direct them to the kind of work internally they are looking to do. Work on their performance now so that they excel in the interim and are sufficiently skilled to make the jump. And then if a jump is necessary, open up that network.

Employees – Take control of your career. Just like you do not need permission to leave, you also do not need permission to **ask** — have the courage to ask management if there are other options internally. Or to tell them that you are unhappy and/or unfulfilled. And be prepared to be told "here is the path to get a particular type of work you want internally," or "here are the skills we need to work on for when you are ready to leave," and, most importantly, "here are performance expectations for you while you are here, and here is how we will help you meet those expectations."

CHAPTER 14

THE LONG GAME

As much as The Long Game is an execution principle of H4L, it's also the outcome when an organization practices the five foundation principles of H4L: Honesty, Inner Awareness, Removing Anxiety, Engaging Alumni, and Demonstration; and when an organization practices the previous four execution principles: Career Conversations, Performance Conversation, The Playbook, and Job Crafting.

**

Lee was pitching a new client for his boutique firm recently. His pitch went the way a lot pitches go for people in his situation:

"I got a big city education, and big city experience, but I'm a local like you, and I charge local prices."

That's a compelling sales pitch!

Now, I know Lee, and this was more than just a client pick-up line. He does great work for his clients and has good references. Needless to say, he won the work. Part of the pitch was the client saw plaintiff-side litigation on the horizon and it would have been more than Lee's firm could handle.

"Not a problem," Lee explained, "I have a friend back in the big city firm, they have lots of bandwidth, and have the capacity to work on contingency."

The client thought this was an excellent idea, as long as his guy, Lee, managed the firm on his behalf. That friend of course was a former colleague of Lee's, and that firm was a former employer. The experience the firm offered him, and the friend's help along the way, put Lee in a position to start his own firm and get the work he wanted, and to pass along the work that wasn't in his wheelhouse to others.

That contingency-fee case could easily be worth north of $1M in fees and percentages.

Lee was worth a lot more as a happy former associate than he would have been as a burnt out bitter former associate.

Now, at least a few partners reading are thinking "Ha! Contingency? That doesn't count."

Really? Because a former colleague of mine down the hall once billed a year's worth of time to a contingency case where the client would likely go bankrupt – even if they won! He got a promotion and full bonus even though the firm did not receive a single penny for his efforts that year. Clearly, firms consider contingency cases valuable.

**

Still need convincing? Let's do some math. Quick, which is greater:

$750,000 or $3,750,000

The first number is 300 billed hours a year at $500 per hour for five years, that's about what you would make on an associate billing them at 2100 hours a year instead of 1800 hours a year for five years. For what it's worth, 1800 per year is very doable for most people who are capable of getting these types of jobs.

2100 isn't crazy, but it starts to wear many down.

The second number is how much a modest corporate client could be worth over five years of getting work. Let me tell you, that second number is probably pretty low. I've seen, and been told stories of, a number of consulting, finance, and accounting contracts, and those multi-year contracts can dwarf $3.75M.

In other words, if one out of every five associates at a firm gets the firm just one client for five years in their entire post firm career, it pays for all five of those associates billing less! Don't forget who decides what firms get corporate work.

**

But beyond the numbers, what about your firm's reputation? Your firm's legacy?

In his 2012 *Bleecher Report* article, John Rozum said the following:

"Since the NFL began in 1920, there have been numerous head coaches with much individual success to their credit.

"Then, there's the coaches who planted a seed and the tree kept growing. It's one area that can really measure a coach's legacy and his impact on pro football."[127]

Let's hit that last line one more time: "It's one area that can really measure a coach's legacy and his impact on pro football."[128] Football has a day every year that journalists refer to as Black Monday. Black Monday is the day after the regular season ends, and is usually accompanied by some number of head coaches, and usually their assistants, being fired. Getting past how messed up that all is, it is shortly followed by a week of interviewing for those teams to find their next head coaches.

If you follow this process you'll hear a number of head coaches say about their own assistants, who they'll lose, things like "If someone doesn't hire this guy, then someone needs to get their head straightened out." I'm sure they'd love to keep great assistants, but they also want what's best for them.

Why don't we hear this more with firms? Wouldn't that be an amazing accolade to say something like, "I've mentored hundreds of associates; in addition to those that are partners here now, 30 have started their own firms and 10 went on to

---

127 Rozum, John. 2012. "Power Ranking The Greatest Coaching Trees In NFL History". *Bleacher Report*. https://bleacherreport.com/articles/1058677-power-ranking-the-greatest-coaching-trees-in-nfl-history#slide0.

128 Ibid.

be Fortune 500 executives." If I heard that as a new associate, I'd be blown away.

There was a time when the first firm I worked for did this. Anytime they had a senior associate come along who they liked, but didn't think they could make partner, they would offer to help that associate get their own firm up and running. I've even heard in one case they gave the associate assistance to build out an office. This is great! You don't have to fire an associate, you've established a mutual relationship with that associate, referrals could go back and forth depending on conflicts and what the firms could or couldn't handle respectively. Why doesn't every firm do this? Better question, why did this firm stop?! They felt threatened is likely why, but there was a change, an associate leaving no longer was a cordial affair.

Al Guido sits at the intersection of sports and business. He is the President of the San Francisco 49ers.

When Al was interviewed by Kim Scott and Russ Laraway for their *Radical Candor* podcast, he spoke extensively about how the level of personal support from organizations he felt and witnessed had a long-term impact on how he tries to handle himself.[129]

---

129 Scott, Kim, and Russ Laraway. 2017. "Ep. 22: It's About Humans, Not Resources". Podcast. *Radical Candor.*

"I worked for a guy by the name of Stephen Jones, who's Jerry Jones' son. And we had a large organization trying to open the [new] Dallas Stadium. We had roughly 80 sales and marketing people there. . . Stephen came through the office one day and he was so embarrassed that he didn't know the people's names."[130]

I think most people wouldn't make a big deal of this. It feels completely understandable to not know these 80 people right away. Especially given that those 80 are just a subset of the organization that he runs. However, Jones clearly felt otherwise.

Guido continued, "He asked me for a face book, he actually called it a book of faces at the time, I didn't really know . . . why he was asking for it when he first reached out. So I gave it to him and I gave him a little bio and background on every single person. . . Two weeks later he had come back and had memorized over half of the individuals that were there. Their names, where they were from, their previous job.

"That was one of the most powerful moments I had ever had in my life. To understand the importance of understanding

---

130 Ibid.

your people and really being at the core of those who effect change in your organization on a daily basis."[131]

Guido later tells Scott and Laraway one of his favorite quotes, which has quickly become a favorite of mine:

"Leadership is not about being in charge. It's about taking care of those in your charge."[132]

At the risk of melodrama, I wonder if some recent views on leadership have at least something to do with a shift in employee harm in the modern office setting typically being better hidden – mental and emotional, rather than life and death.

There are certainly any number of examples of horrible physical peril for employees throughout history in the name of profit – forced labor, sweat shops, factories etc. But there are also great examples where true leadership is shown, and the focus is on the people involved.

Specifically, I'm thinking of historic and modern military, and the historic shipping industry. Both have traditional leadership chains of command, both have significant physical

131 Ibid.
132 Ibid.

risk inherent in the job. In both cases, the first indicator of mission success is whether everyone makes it back alive. Then, assess to what degree the actual mission was a success.

Literally taking care of those in your charge.

But there continues to be resistance in the modern age. In my limited experience, and in the experience of many I know, the corporate goal is to grind out as much as humanly possible out of associates until they burn out, and then replace them with fresh blood. But again, why?

Thankfully, Guido had a different experience, saying: "I've been lucky enough [where] I've been hired and people have always had my best interests at heart . . . They never put the team or the organization before my best interests. Because I think they always felt that if they were serving my best interest I would be serving the team."[133]

This makes a lot of sense to me. If the skills that will help an associate start their own firm, or go in-house, or whatever, are the same skills that will help them bill more hours more efficiently, then why not outwardly help that associate meet their goals?

---

133 Ibid.

If the only reason an associate feels they need to leave is because they want to bill a little less and just crank away, why not work that out for them at your firm?

If an associate wants to start their own firm one day, and wants to work on business development, why not mentor them? Maybe they end up building enough business that it makes sense to stay.

If an associate wants to go in-house, or work for the government, why not make arrangements for that early. Why wouldn't it be helpful to get four, five or more years out of a future FDA specialist, or indemnity specialist, or startup corporate governance specialist?

These associates are still profitable assets even if they leave.

They're going to leave anyway. They'll want to go in-house; they'll want to start their own shop; they won't have enough business to make partner; they want better hours at a smaller competitor; who knows. But they're leaving. So why not help make them the best possible candidate for when they leave?

The better they are, when they are there, is better for the firm!

This is brings us right back to the coaching tree discussion.

It's clear that Guido agrees with me, saying, "It's our job to have those conversations around goal setting and making sure that people feel as though they're being pushed at their current opportunity. And when that current opportunity either isn't good enough for them or they feel like they've achieved their results or there's an opening maybe at another team, it's my job to make sure I'm pushing for those people to get those opportunities because I've always viewed it as not only helping that individual; it's helping the 49ers."[134]

So, right off the bat Guido is thinking employee first but not just because he wants what's best for them, he does of course, but because that aligns with what's best, long term, for the 49ers.

He finished with this: "I want to be known, and the organization wants to be known, as a leading brand in the sports world. To do that, it means having people say 'wow the 49ers have fantastic people and a fantastic culture. Look at all the people that currently work there and that used to work there.'"[135]

Many firms touch on this. Management consulting firms are better than law firms here. Likely due to the perception

---

134 Ibid.
135 Ibid.

that there are just more in-house jobs for ex-management consultants than there are for lawyers. Yet, law firms do touch on this as well. You mostly see it from the firm where a partner goes.

"We're really expanding our criminal defense practice with this superstar partner from white shoe firm!"

But rarely do you hear, "We're so excited for young gun partner, who will be opening white show firm's white collar practice in Los Angeles. We know young gun will make the firm family proud!"

Guido does have that pride though:

"And so I'm proud of that tree. In sports they call that the coaching tree. Here we call it the executive tree. I'm very proud to say that these people started here and now have gone on to use that philosophy at other teams."

**

Firms regularly play the long game with clients. They cut bills with little fight, they let clients go months and years without paying, they front them money for out of pocket expenses, and they do countless free work.

Why?

So when those clients are paying, they keep paying, and for as long a period of time as possible. Firms also regularly play the long game with existing corporate contacts. In addition, to all the freebies they give the corporations on their behalf, they wine and dine them, give them office space when they're in town, and on and on.

Yet, for some reason firms consistently fail to play the long game with future clients – the future clients that are sitting in their building, grinding away at their work.

When you hire associates for life, you establish lifetime relationships with those future clients; you expand your coaching tree.

You cement your legacy.

**

How each of the three groups can make The Long Game work.

Culture – Make it clear that what your alumni do in the industry and beyond is just as important as what your current employees and organization is doing within your four walls.

Managers – Every interaction with an associate, from the time they step foot in the door as a summer, through their first day of associate orientation is an encounter with a future partner, a future collaborator, or a future client. When you are having performance conversations, and career conversations, and consider what knowledge you'd want a future partner to have, or a future client to have.

Employee – View yourself as the long-term asset that you are, whether you are a superstar, a rockstar, or just an associate trying to keep up. Know that you are valuable to the firm now, and in the future, and consider that when you are having career conversations and performance conversations. Make a plan to job craft and use the playbook to determine who might help you best. You're playing the long game as well.

BIBLIOGRAPHY

INTRODUCTION

"Professional Services Industry Spotlight | Selectusa.Gov". 2019. Selectusa.Gov. https://www.selectusa.gov/professional-services-industry-united-states.

CHAPTER 1

"Definition Of FUNGIBLE". 2019. Merriam-Webster.Com. https://www.merriam-webster.com/dictionary/fungible.

Hoffman, Reid, Chris Yeh, and Ben Casnocha. 2013. The Alliance. London: HarperCollins.

Lencioni, Patrick. 2012. The Advantage. San Francisco: Jossey-Bass.

Martindale, Nick. 2014. "Partnership Management Model Outdated?". Economia.Icaew.Com. https://economia.icaew.com/features/march-2014/shift-away-from-partnership-model.

Porter, Michael, and Victor Millar. 1985. "How Information Gives You Competitive Advantage". Harvard Business Review. https://hbr.org/1985/07/how-information-gives-you-competitive-advantage.

CHAPTER 2

Bort, Julie. 2014. "This Guy Was Fired And Sued By His Employer, So He Launched A Startup And Got Sweet Revenge". Business Insider. https://www.businessinsider.com/modus-ceo-from-jobless-to-success-2014-4.

"Deloitte Global Millennial Survey 2018". 2018. Deloitte. https://www2.deloitte.com/global/en/pages/about-deloitte/articles/millennialsurvey.html.

Hoffman, Reid, Chris Yeh, and Ben Casnocha. 2013. The Alliance. London: HarperCollins.

Ruggeri, Amanda. 2017. "What Everyone Gets Wrong About 'Millennial Snowflakes'". Bbc.Com. http://www.bbc.com/capital/story/20171003-millennials-are-the-generation-thats-fun-to-hate.

CHAPTER 3

Dweck, Carol. 2016. Mindset. New York: Random House.

Hoffman, Reid, Chris Yeh, and Ben Casnocha. 2013. The Alliance. London: HarperCollins.

"The Power Of Vulnerability | Brené Brown". 2019. Youtube. https://www.youtube.com/watch?v=iCvmsMzlF7o.

Westfall, Brian. 2019. "Why Honesty Is The Secret Ingredient Of Successful Organizations". Software Advice. Accessed June 30. https://www.softwareadvice.com/resources/why-honesty-is-the-secret-ingredient-of-successful-organizations/.

"Why Good Leaders Make You Feel Safe | Simon Sinek". 2019. Youtube. https://www.youtube.com/watch?v=lmyZMtPVodo.

CHAPTER 4

Dweck, Carol. 2016. Mindset. New York: Random House.

Rock, Chris. 2014. The Howard Stern Show. Interview by Howard Stern. Radio. Sirius XM.

CHAPTER 5

Estrich, Susan. 2004. How To Get Into Law School. New York: Riverhead Books.

Pysh, Preston, and Stig Broderson. 2018. "TIP187: The Culture Code W/ Daniel Coyle (Business Podcast)". Podcast. We Study Billionaires – The Investor Podcast.

CHAPTER 6

Arnold, Paul. 2018. "Alumni Center". Mckinsey & Company. Accessed August. https://alumni.mckinsey.com/public_content/500179854.

"BCG Alumni Network | BCG Careers". 2019. Https://Www.Bcg.Com. https://www.bcg.com/en-us/careers/working-at-bcg/alumni-network.aspx.

"Gone But Not Forgotten". 2019. The Economist. https://www.economist.com/business/2014/03/01/gone-but-not-forgotten#ampf=undefined.

"Seven Top Tips From Corporate Alumni Leaders – Conenza". 2019. Conenza. https://www.conenza.com/insights/seven-top-tips-corporate-alumni-leaders/.

CHAPTER 7

Grant, Adam. 2018. "How To Trust People You Don't Like". Podcast. Work Life.

"Full Transcript: Kim Scott And Her Book 'Radical Candor' Live Onstage For Recode Decode". 2017. Vox. https://www.vox.com/2017/4/13/15295070/transcript-kim-scott-book-radical-candor-live-onstage-recode-decode.

Pysh, Preston, and Stig Broderson. 2018. "TIP187: The Culture Code W/ Daniel Coyle (Business Podcast)". Podcast. We Study Billionaires – The Investor Podcast.

"Trust Fail: Fails Of The Week (December 2018) | Failarmy". 2018. Youtube. https://www.youtube.com/watch?v=1UJeriMDPyk.

CHAPTER 8

"BCG Alumni Network | BCG Careers". 2019. Https://Www.Bcg.Com. https://www.bcg.com/en-us/careers/working-at-bcg/alumni-network.aspx.

"Gone But Not Forgotten". 2019. The Economist. https://www.economist.com/business/2014/03/01/gone-but-not-forgotten#ampf=undefined.

Rock, Chris. 2014. The Howard Stern Show. Interview by Howard Stern. Radio. Sirius XM

CHAPTER 9

"Full Transcript: Kim Scott And Her Book 'Radical Candor' Live Onstage For Recode Decode". 2017. Vox. https://www.vox.com/2017/4/13/15295070/transcript-kim-scott-book-radical-candor-live-onstage-recode-decode.

Grant, Adam. 2018. "The Problem With All-Stars". Podcast. Work Life.

Scott, Kim, and Russ Laraway. 2017. "Ep. 23: Can I Give Feedback To Peers? Should I?". Podcast. Radical Candor.

CHAPTER 10

Schmidt, Emily. 2017. "Why I Told My Boss I Was Thinking About Quitting.". Thinkgrowth.Org. https://thinkgrowth.org/why-i-told-my-boss-i-was-thinking-about-quitting-d117db4a93f4.

Scott, Kim, and Russ Laraway. 2017. "Ep. 5: Career Conversations". Podcast. Radical Candor.

CHAPTER 12

Grant, Adam. 2018. "Your Hidden Personality". Podcast. Work Life.

CHAPTER 14

Rozum, John. 2012. "Power Ranking The Greatest Coaching Trees In NFL History". Bleacher Report. https://bleacherreport.com/articles/1058677-power-ranking-the-greatest-coaching-trees-in-nfl-history#slide0.

Scott, Kim, and Russ Laraway. 2017. "Ep. 22: It's About Humans, Not Resources". Podcast. Radical Candor.

CPSIA information can be obtained
at www.ICGtesting.com
Printed in the USA
FSHW011824240719
60363FS

2 370009 47091